PADEN HUGHES

How a Simple Daily Habit Increased My Health, Wealth and Happiness

Published and distributed by Merack Publishing.

Library of Congress Control Number 2022914813
Hughes, Paden
Take Two: How a Simple Daily Habit Increased My Health, Wealth and Happiness

ISBNS: 978-1-957048-31-4 Paperback
ISBNS: 978-1-957048-32-1 eBook
ISBNS: 978-1-957048-33-8 Hardcover

dedication

This book, it's words and message is dedicated to all the fierce, intuitive women in my bloodline and beyond who were told to be more gentle, less ambitious and to dim their magnetism and magic to meet approval. To the women whose wisdom, passion, and strength flow through my veins and poured through me as I wrote these pages. Sharing my truth in the pages of this book healed a part of me and in doing so represents a new beginning for the women who came before me and will live on after me.

CONTENTS

prologue
CHAPTER ZERO

Full disclosure: I am not the kind of person who ever reads a prologue, much less a preface. If my editor hadn't told me to write one and what type of content goes into it, *Take Two* would have just started with Chapter Zero typed on a blank page, and I would have stared at it for a solid month.

This is one of a gazillion things I didn't know about writing a book, including what type of work goes into an endeavor like this. My genuine apologies to every author I ever bought a book from and skipped right into Chapter 1. You deserved better from me.But here I am writing a damned introduction to a book I never intended to write.

This book is about a year and a half in my life—one filled with stories that really should only be told to your closest girlfriends after a bottle of wine. I didn't expect to share a lot of what you'll read here with the world. In fact, I can think of about ten people I hope don't pick up this book and recognize the facts that point to them, even if the names don't. Ambitious as I am, and I am, I thought this story would make an entertaining TED talk one day. I didn't see a book in it until my mentor suggested I might reach more of the women who needed my message in book form. I honestly feel bad for whoever has to determine which shelf this book belongs on in a bookstore. Seriously. It's not a traditional self-help book. This book doesn't prescribe a 5-step process for unlimited success. Rather, it shows you what can happen when you stop doing and start being. Parts of *Take Two* could be categorized as spirituality. It is a story about personal enlightenment. But I'm not sure which religion in the modern world would ever agree with all the perspectives I share here. It's a book rooted in my own lived experience, which comes with a lens of privilege and gives voice to situations that share my singular viewpoint only. I guess that makes *Take Two* part memoir as well, one that takes the pithy phrase "make your mess your message" literally.

This is also a book about what happens when a stressed-out CEO of a nonessential business, in the middle of a pandemic, with two kids under four, actually does the unthinkable: takes two hours a day to find a source of joy—and then does it every day (minus the five days we thought my husband had COVID-19) for a year. It's pretty much a documentary in a book. Oh good, a fourth genre—book shelvers everywhere are going to love me. Take Two is about making time to step out of your demanding life to listen to the demands of your soul. Before taking two hours a day, I had convinced myself that I was living a good life. I was over here doing this, doing that, always busy, always "on". I knew I felt things. I knew I had opinions about things. I was even a little pissed off about some stuff. But until this year, I didn't give myself the thinking space to sort through things I'd worried about, stressed about, or just straight-up avoided. I hadn't given myself the tools to figure out how to make my life align with what my deepest desires were. Beyond that, a year before I wouldn't have had the courage to tell the stories I do in this boo—these parts of my fragile ego—or to put my name to the rants I air here.

A year ago I still believed that...

- At my core, I was a fighter, strong, fierce, and tough-minded.
- My decisions are sounder when based in logic only.
- If I couldn't accept Christianity, I was unlikely to be connected to God.
- Success comes from hard work, period.
- I could have it all and should be able to have it all.

Until I took two hours a day, I didn't completely understand *these* things, though.

- I am perceptive and an intuitive reader of people and business scenarios.
- I am a deep thinker and feeler, and those are my superpowers.
- I have performed for love in most areas of my life.
- I have been angry deep down.
- I am and have always been a spiritual seeker.
- I am willing to spend a lot of time and money publishing a somewhat embarrassing book to get a message out that I believe in to support people I came here to help.

Oh shit, does that make this an inspirational book? How many genres is that?

Well, if reading *Take Two* inspires you, then I will feel every piece of criticism I faced down to bring this book to life was all worth it. Thank you for taking a risk on a yet unknown author trying to bring a bit more joy to the world.

I invite you to pour yourself a glass of wine and start at the beginning:

my breaking point,

my cry for help, and

my reckoning as a type A, American mom.

introduction
WHEN IT HITS THE FAN

"Let our hearts be stretched out in compassion toward others,
for everyone is walking his or her own difficult path."
- Dieter F. Uchtdorf

Stillness. So hard to come by. There I was smack dab in the middle of a rare moment of ... peace? No, that's wishful. It wasn't a sense of peace I felt. It was a loneliness, a deep isolation. I sat there in my bathrobe, ready for bed but unable to go there.

My mind was restless. If I didn't clear it, I'd lay awake for hours with my thoughts spiraling. I needed to get my thoughts out of my head so they wouldn't spiral that night while I tried to sleep. To myself. For myself. I needed to say things I hated to admit to others—expose my truest burdens.

I grabbed the only tool I could think of, my iPhone. I created a new note and started to type, hunched over on the bathroom floor.

JANUARY 29, 2020

This has been the hardest six months of my life. Looking back, here's all the shit that went down.

- *I didn't take a maternity leave after baby #2, and Michael only got one week off. My anxiety was insane the weekend before I had to parent two kids solo by day and be CEO at night.*

- *I struggled to adjust to life with two kids, two nap schedules, two different ways of eating, two sets of needs. Someone always needing me and zero alone time. I was ready to throat punch anyone that told me "just sleep when the baby does." Obviously you can't when you have a toddler AND a baby.*

- *I battled postpartum depression for four months after Jackson was born—not the "baby blues" everyone tried to tell me. I knew damn well it was full-blown, bat-shit-crazy, postpartum depression. I remember figuring it out one day in the Fall when I was making breakfast, and a song came on, and I melted to the ground of my kitchen floor in my bathrobe and just sobbed … I felt numb, depleted, irritable as hell, and most of the time stared off in a daze wondering, How has my life come to this point? Too many days I felt trapped in my life, like someone being waterboarded with the "American Dream." Not fucking baby blues.*

- *Someone from our past, an addict and someone I'm scared of being around my children, moved into a halfway house two blocks away from us, and my husband and I didn't feel safe walking the streets by our house with the kids, so we stayed trapped in the house for months.*

- *Kennedy, at age 2.5 years old, developed a stutter as soon as Jackson was born. This retraumatized my husband, who battled a stutter himself growing up after the trauma of losing his mom at 6-months-old. We didn't know why she developed it or how to get rid of it, so at 3 am I Googled everything I could think of in the hopes of becoming a speech pathologist in between nighttime feedings.*

- *I haven't slept more than two hours in a row in the last six months; my brain fog at work started to cost the business because I couldn't keep facts in my brain long enough to remember which urgent/important tasks needed to be done, or who I'd paid or hadn't.*
- *We started creating an online coaching certification program, and my husband needed help writing scripts about super smart movement science (of which I knew zilch, and somehow I had to make it sound fun and memorable), and we rallied in the only hours we had kid free: 10 pm - 12 midnight every damn day for six months.*
- *We made the single worst investment we'd ever made to date, putting six figures into a digital marketing "superstar" whose only real achievement was the con job he played on us that sucked every savings account, line of credit, and rainy day fund we had. We bet the farm and crossed our fingers that our course would skyrocket.*
- *And I'd just gotten back from my grandmother's funeral. She died out of the blue, and it was a deep loss for me personally.*

But at least in 2019 we hit 7-figures in our business and found out that put our single location fitness facility in the top 5% of US gyms for revenue with the best, long-term clients and a business that was getting invited to speak on top fitness podcasts to share our success story. How had we been able to retain a workforce for an average of five years, when the industry average was six months? How did we hit 7-figures in the small California college town of San Luis Obispo? How did we manage to build a gym membership that primarily served baby boomers and had a churn rate of under 3%? And of course, how did we do it as a married couple with little kids?

I mean, that was all the Enneagram 3 in me wanted to focus on. That was what I'd been sacrificing for this whole time. That's the side I wanted people to see, not the secret cost of hustle culture, soldiering on, getting no breaks as a mom-entrepreneur, negotiating insurance policies while getting pumped with Pitocin at the hospital delivering baby number two.

I mean it was 2020, we'd just celebrated a decade in business and business was booming… despite me being an internal shit show.

I finished my note in my iPhone. I could squeeze out some sympathy for my inner shit show. It had been hard. I could do hard things. The list proved it. I breathed out. Thank God I was putting 2019 behind me, and 2020 should be so much better.

And now as I write this book, that phrase is so damned laughable. because what you know as you read this, and I didn't at the time, was what 2020 ushered in.

COVID-19 was weeks away from arriving. The pandemic hit. Executive orders went out to shelter-in-place for "two weeks," which snowballed into two years of restrictions. And 2020 became the year where we'd essentially be forced to shutter our fitness gym for ten straight months with zero dollars in the bank, no savings. Our landlord's expecting full rent, our staff counting on their jobs, and us wondering if our clients would stick with us.

The shit hadn't even hit the fan when I wrote that iPhone list in the bathroom.

I will spare you what it meant to be the CEO of a company that was branded "nonessential" and forced to fully close for months and pivot twelve different times depending on the level of "partially open" we were required to obey. Pivots required endless capital, and the situations were never quite good enough for all our clients and required pep talks to our team, as we all suffered from change fatigue and our own mental health navigating the pandemic.

But as bad as all this was, we were a hell of a lot better off than most of our industry. By August 2020, reports were coming out that 25% of fitness facilities permanently closed and that an estimated 78% of personal trainers and fitness coaches were unemployed. Most fitness goers had developed new loyalty with global brands like Peloton, casting doubt as to what the fitness industry's recovery would even look like post-pandemic.

But we pushed hard. We didn't stop We kept evolving. Our pace of innovation was our best defense. We pivoted our entire business in three days, a week before shelter-in-place orders went out, saving 95% of our memberships. We kept the team together, paid in full, and financially we ended 2020 with only 8% less revenue than 2019. I also used the shelter-in-place time to finally bond with Jackson. He was 8-months-old when the pandemic hit. At the time, I beat myself up for not being emotionally connected to him as a mom who should have had a six- month maternity leave. Well, guess what? Self-employed people don't have that luxury. I spent more time taking my stuttering 3-year-old daughter out of the house for "special girls' time". She started to get better. And Michael and I felt energized and excited to be working closer together than we ever had.

When I look back on the first half of the pandemic, I feel so damned proud of our team and what I personally overcame. How I chose gratitude, and I credit it almost entirely to the journey I've documented in this book and my sacred habit of taking two hours to be alone and recharge.

I see the pandemic as two parts.

The epic survival full of pivots and innovation and the team beating the odds, our members grateful that we continued to find ways to show up and serve. In fact, I got so mentally and soulfully aligned, one night Michael asked me, "Do you even need to do two hours anymore?"

I considered it. Maybe he was right. What if the two hours had been a lesson learned, and now I knew how to quickly snap myself out of a funk or reduce my anxiety?

I decided I loved it too much to give it up, but that maybe I should "test it out" and be more relaxed about it to see what would happen.

I guess the Universe heard me and ushered in a new line up of "tests". Here's how it went down.

In June 2021, we'd finally seen new growth in our business. It was the first month I hadn't had to pull money from our government funding to float the business. It felt like hope. But in July, phase two of the pandemic reared its head in the name of the Delta variant. Fear rose as the surge grew, and with the fear, a lot of anger, a lot of blaming and further polarization.

We lost $20K in July. Holy shit, that snapped me out of my zen vibes.

$20K? 20 fucking K? I had been proud that 18 months into this pandemic we still had 50% of all the government funding untouched. But shit, at that rate we'd be out of money in five months. Five months? That scared me. So I clung to my two hours a day like it was the only buoy in the ocean keeping me afloat.

I manifested. I walked in nature. I danced to tribal music by the ocean. Every time I did, it revived me for another 24-hour cycle. It was pretty much my daily vitamin of hope.

Then August hit. The COVID-19 Delta variant was in full swing, and all the hope in our community from June disappeared and was replaced by fear and anger, blame and hate, and finger-pointing. The real variant of the virus was how the doom and gloom morphed for each of us producing versions of ourselves in survival mode, trapped in our own mental health crisis.

As an empath, I absorb energy from others. It stays with me and builds over time if I don't clear it. At this point, I was consulting for several businesses on top of running my two. All of them were in different industries, positioned for greatness, and by mid-August, every one of them had business-threatening issues. Their problems felt like mine. I started to feel enmeshed in their partnership tensions, and their cashflow issues and random bouts of "bad luck" were starting to fuck with me. My hope started to wane, and my two hours were harder to prioritize.

Then we lost $25k in August. I knew it by the 15th. That's how bad it was. I had just moved $20k out of our reserves July 26th, and three weeks later I already needed another $25k.

MORE PAINFUL THAN ASKING FOR HELP

At this point everyone and everything around me was in a full-blown state of survival, and somehow everyone was looking to me for the right strategy, the genius move, and you want to know what I came up with? Asking for help. It came to me on one of my walks, a sense that there is a deep benevolence in humanity, a reminder that there is no shame in asking for help. In fact, it's a sign of strength. I mean, how many of us love helping our people and businesses we love? It always brings me joy. I love helping. But there was one problem. I hated being the one to get help. Now in a society that condemns burnout, while rewarding all the actions that create burnout....

... it's no different than asking for help.

We share cute memes on social media that asking for help is so important. Things like "No woman is an island." We know it like a test taker who crammed for exams at midnight knows a quick fact, but we forget it as soon as it becomes our turn.

I felt my intuition had spoken, and so that night I decided to email my people, the ones I felt had my back, loved me and could always be counted on.

I emailed the closest people to me, those I'd known for a lifetime. For someone who loves to write, I could barely type out the first paragraph. A huge emotion surged up in me. Shame. So much shame in having to ask for help. Like I'm a failure to have to need help.

Michael looked up at me across the table, seeing my tears, and reminded me every business owner at one point or another has to reach into their network to ask for referrals to their business. But that wasn't what this email was for me. It was about being in a vulnerable situation and asking for a favor. It was hard, but I did it. I cried my eyes out writing the stupid thing. I finally hit send and went to bed, believing I'd sent out the Hail Mary I needed. Help was on the way. I finally took everyone up on all the times they'd said, "If you ever need anything, let us know."

I must have checked my email every hour for days. After a week, here is what I'd received:

- I got a couple of response A's: I'm so sorry. I'll pray for you. Unfortunately, this isn't a really convenient time for me.
- I got response B: I got your email. How are the kids? How is consulting? Good? Okay, at least something is going well in your life. (Which felt a LOT like toxic positivity.)
- I got response C: I was worried when I got your email. I thought there is nothing worse than Paden losing her company. but then I realized what good is it to gain the world and lose your soul. Paden, I have to ask you, where are you with Jesus? I would hate for you not to be in Heaven with me.
- I also got several response D's: Let's brainstorm some solutions. I'm available to advise if you need it.
- And sadly, the vast majority of the people I reached out to never responded.
- Then the kicker: Your email wasn't compelling enough for me to respond.

I was stupified. THIS was the result of humbling myself and bringing my circle into my mess so they could help? What is wrong with people? Do I have to lose a limb before anyone sees me as in need?

No, it's clear you're just not worth the effort to them.

Shut up Bitchy Brittany.

I will shout out three responses: One person bought an online membership and congratulated me for having the courage to ask for help. Another sent a sweet note and shared on her social media how amazing our workout programs were. Then my personal network MVP, who already at the start of the pandemic purchased online members to help us with cashflow, offered to connect me with an online nutritionist to potentially partner with them in selling virtual fitness to her clients.

But like most things in life, when you're in survival mode, which responses stand out? The helpful ones or the ones that confirmed a big childhood wound, "You're not a priority." I learned at that moment that the only thing worse than asking for help was asking for it and not getting it. I was hurt. Then my dysfunctional pattern to turn hurt into anger resurrected in full force.

All I'd been looking for was … 10 new referrals that would have snowballed into 50 new memberships. I wasn't looking for enough money to afford my dream red Tesla with white interior. I was looking for a bone to help me revitalize the business that had been on the chopping block for 16 months. The handle I had on my mindset and emotions was giving way. I couldn't think. I couldn't work, so I took my two hours right there in the middle of the work day, and after 10 months of being all zen and spiritual, anger felt so out of place. Thankfully, I had practiced how to get rid of it. Compassion meditation. Whenever I was angry at someone who had hurt me, this never failed to help me calm down and get my heart beating with love. I did a compassion meditation, specifically visualizing the person who said my ask for help wasn't compelling enough to warrant a response. Damn! They had it coming. I was going to compassion meditate on their ass so hard it would shake them to their bones.

And I did. I sent them ALL the love. All the earnest intention I had in me to not be a source of pain in their life, and, you know what, it worked!

In 20 minutes, I wasn't mad anymore. I was sending loving energy to this person with the purest of intentions. Despite the vindictiveness I cruised into the mediation with, I exited it with so much love and understanding. Holy shit, this is powerful. Then I had a huge epiphany in the form of a quiet inner voice, "What if every response to my ask for help mirrored each person's internal response to their own needs? What if everyone had done the best they could? Is that MORE true than believing that they don't care about you?"

For those who directed me to God, they did because they do not ask humans for help. Their sole source of help is God, so they directed me there. I didn't have to like it or agree, but it was done out of love from their place of truth.

For those who acknowledged their own overwhelm and being too busy right now to help, were they trying to hold their own boundaries in their own season of overwhelm? Was their honesty intended to hurt?

For the one who couldn't acknowledge the discomfort of my email, but instead tried to steer me into grasping for anything positive to hang their hat on … how many times do they push down the negative in their life and put on blinders so they can only see the positive? Maybe they felt comforted by that and just wanted to share that with me?

For those who didn't even respond, how many times do they deny their needs and just push it away? Or just maybe, they didn't see the email at all.

And for the one who said it wasn't compelling enough … did this person believe their needs are compelling enough to merit acting on them?

Without "knowing," I knew. It rang true in my gut.

That single thought removed every last ounce of judgment I had. I cleared it all in 20 minutes, not two hours. It felt so powerful and transformative. I got into my car and headed home to dinner happy and deeply thankful that in the midst of a shit storm, my two hours had shaken me out of angry victim mode into blissful gratitude.

Thank you, Universe, for that lesson.

TESTING POSITIVE

We were mid Delta variant and still losing money hand over fist when we got this text from one of our coaches.

"My wife just tested positive for COVID." Shit. This was worse.

We pulled this team member off the schedule immediately, hoping he'd test negative. Thankfully, by some miracle, he'd only coached two or three sessions in two days. The exposure, should he test positive, was minimal.

But we all took tests as a team to be sure. Thank God every one came back negative.

We waited Thursday and all day Friday. Then I got two texts Friday evening. "My test was positive, and I'm starting to have symptoms. It's getting hard to breathe."

"Hey Paden, a client (Jeff) just texted me that he tested positive for COVID and was apologizing for exposing us."

Saturday came and went. I was bracing for bad news. I had an instinct that it wasn't the end of it. Sunday I asked everyone to retest so we could know how full of a team we actually had going into our work week.

Two more coaches tested positive. Eighteen months, that's how long we'd gone with no case on the team. Now I had fifty percent of my coaching staff out for 10 days, and a client. We made the hard choice to close in-person training for the entire week and to train virtually.

Monday morning I took two hours right away. I went to the ocean, danced my heart out, and found a repose of peace. Sitting out there on a secret bluff, safe from tourists, watching the water ebb and flow and all the birds scavenge food, I remembered once again that when in nature there is always more that is in control than is out of control. I felt peaceful.

I walked into the office knowing it would be a hard day. It was a bloodbath. Our customer service team was getting blasted with more accusations, more demands to know who was and wasn't vaccinated on the team, when they tested positive, etc. So far, what I know to be true is that as a "nonessential" entrepreneur in COVID, you're damned if you do and damned if you don't. There are so few win-win scenarios. Every two days the rest of the team was doing PCR tests. All week we waited to hear who else was sick, but then we got two more positive tests. We now had one able-bodied coach by Labor Day Weekend, and we'd lost thousands of dollars the week we closed, and I'd found out, after promising the team we'd cover their emergency sick leave, that the government didn't have the regulation dialed in, and so there would be no relief for our team members' emergency sick leave. We'd be paying for that too.

To make it worse, I'd randomly signed into LinkedIn and saw a post of our best friend sharing that his business had been named one of Inc's Fastest Growing Companies. Fuck. Seriously? I fell into petty comparison for a hot minute. You see, before the pandemic, our businesses revenue was comparable. Yet in the same 12 weeks that shuttered our business, they'd doubled theirs. They now hit such a winning streak that they got awarded for their fast growth, and we had just closed our business for an entire week because half the team tested positive for COVID … all breakout cases. I felt a little like the kid who picked the short stick.

All week I'd been finding an hour to walk and listen to my heart reassure me I was safe. I was loved, and I would be supported through this season. It was the lifeblood I needed each day to keep facing the next.

THE TEST: FIVE DAYS NO TWO HOURS

Then, on the Friday of Labor Day weekend, Michael tested positive for COVID. I canceled the cleaners, the nannies, pre-school, and found myself at home with a COVID-positive husband and two kids, and four consulting clients and two businesses to run and no help. In that moment, there wasn't even time to take a walk around the block. We all had to self-isolate. No two hours per day, not when I needed it the most. Not even 8-10 pm I needed that time to work to catch up., and God knows why—on top of that I decided it was my shot at potty training my two year old son. Why not add one more thing to the plate?!?

In those five days I felt old patterns and old beliefs creep back in,and my mindset caved. I went into low-vibe, don't-give-a-shit-about anything, just-can't-do-it-any-more mode.

Then we caught a lucky break, and Michael got two negative PCR tests on Tuesday.

It turned out he had gotten a false positive over the counter test, and the original team member would be done with quarantine Tuesday after Labor Day. We could reopen, and the day we did, I took my two hours, and I realized something powerful: after five days without taking two hours for myself, I done some backsliding, but I hadn't lost it yet. I hadn't yelled, snapped, or been snarky, and it had been three times worse than when I wrote that iPhone note I wrote at the beginning of this Introduction.

I wasn't in a test; I was the test, and I had made it through. The universe had given me the answer before I started the test. I was still standing upright. I stood there in my kitchen knee deep in appreciation. What a contrast, standing here upright, a survivor, thinking back to a year ago when I'd hit the kitchen floor.

PART I

breakdown to breakthrough

"When you're powerful in your dysfunction, it's hard to leave."
- Allyson Byrd

chapter 1

KITCHEN FLOOR

"I'm sorry, but I know what looks correct, and this situation looks incorrect!"
- David Rose, *Schitt's Creek*

God, I'm tired. What's wrong with me?

It's 2 o'clock in the afternoon, and I feel like it is 10 pm. Since becoming a mom, I was definitely more efficient with any uninterrupted block of time, but my energy and memory were a constant liability to progress. There I am, staring blankly at my computer screen trying to care about the marketing plan I'm putting together, but all I want to do is gaze into oblivion … and experience a life of zero thoughts. Not in the cool spiritual guru way. No, in the, I've-officially-fried-my-brain-and-have-nothing-to-contribute-to-this-life kind of way.

Zoned out. No thoughts.

This energy lull was happening more and more often. In fact, it felt oddly nice to be completely numb in front of my split-screen monitor. No one asking me to make a decision about how the next COVID restriction would impact the business. No one asking me to pay them for babysitting on Venmo. No kid asking for a snack 30 minutes before dinner. No one asking me what we're having for dinner. (Hell if I knew, anyway.)

I was fidgeting with Meena, the Beanie Baby thing with the enormous glittery eyes that my daughter adored and had run out of the house that morning to give me before I left for work saying, "Mama! Here, take this to remember me by." I'd felt that familiar pang of mom guilt as I kissed her goodbye and sent her back in the house to play with her nanny. I pushed that memory away for a moment. Happier in the void.

Sitting there in my messy office with piles of unfinished to-do lists, playing with Meena. It was almost peaceful just sitting there, in my office. The one place I could be alone. At 34-years-old, this had become my notion of "quiet time." I looked down at my phone. 4:05. *Shit, I'm supposed to be home at 4! Keke, our Tuesday nanny, was going to be so annoyed. Why do I always push it to the last damn minute? Is it really THAT hard to leave early? I mean, all I was doing was staring at the damn computer screen wasting time.*

I threw my shit into my grocery bag of a purse and hurried to my car, trying to ignore the voice of Bitchy Brittany in my head...

- *Why are you always so fucking late?*
- *Aren't you a CEO? Shouldn't you know how to show up for shit on time?*
- *Why not just leave early? Why do you always insist on working right past the time you need to be somewhere?*
- *Are you going to be like this when your kids grow up and have to be picked up from school or have a dance recital? Are you going to be THAT parent, the one who's always fucking late? Is that how you want your kids to remember you?*

I looked at the clock again. I was for sure going to be 15 minutes late. Usually, at this point, my brain reverts back to childhood, where I'm worried I'm going to disappoint someone, and I start frantically searching for excuses.

… I hit all the red lights.

I used that one last week.

… There was a super slow person who couldn't figure out how to turn left into oncoming traffic.

I live in San Luis Obispo, not L.A. There is never traffic.

… My meeting went long.

Was I seriously going to pretend I was in a meeting?

That's how I usually spent my drive going home. Five minutes of late shaming and then mentally feeling like a teenager after curfew.

But today was different.

Bitchy Brittany's voice sounded further away, like it was fading, and within three minutes of that drive, I was slouched in my seat, barely able to read the street signs as I drove. Good thing I could drive my usual route by muscle memory, if I had to.

What's wrong with me? What is going on?

I struggled to keep my eyes open. Seriously, it felt like I'd have to bench press my eyelids open to see anything. Just one more block till the turn. My eyelids closed, in slow motion. I sank into a glorious pool of ease.

I jerked my head in an emergency response.

Holy shit!

I swerved away from the tree in front of me, getting back onto the road, and cut off the car in the lane next to me, narrowly avoiding clipping them.

WTF! Did I just fall asleep?

Am I still driving?

Did I hurt anyone?

Am I still in the same lane?

Did anyone see that?

I rolled down the windows. It was okay. I was almost home. I was fine. Clearly.

What the fuck is wrong with you? I felt like someone siphoned all my energy, and I was empty. I pulled the car over and closed my eyes for a couple minutes. I tried to coach myself, but all I could think is:

What the fuck is wrong with you?

Snap out of this. You're better than this.

This isn't you.

Wake the fuck up. Get home. You have kids waiting on you. Nannies pissed at you. You don't get to close your eyes, not for hours. I parked. Still no energy.

I don't remember the walk to the front door. I just remember pulling myself together to manage a smile to Keke and mumbling that I'm sorry I'm late again. No excuses, that was too much effort. She was pretending not to be annoyed, but in less than two seconds, she was out the front door.

I put my purse down and my kids bombarded me. My toddler was crying, trying to grab for my boobs to nurse. My 4-year-old was whining about how hungry she is. I shuffled them to the kitchen. They were talking over each other, competing for my attention, but their voices seemed far away.

Then it went black. I opened my eyes and was staring at a ceiling, lying on a hardwood floor. There was blurry light coming from a sky light. And some green plants hanging over gray cabinets.

Where am I?

I notice some pots and pans stacked on a drying rack. I must be in a kitchen.

Why am I on the ground?

This is strange.

I tried to get off the ground, but I couldn't. I've got nothing. Ziltch. Can't move.

Weird.

I try again.

Still nothing.

"Mama?" I knew that voice. Kennedy, my daughter. I knew I must be in my kitchen.

"Mama, what's wrong with you?" my daughter asked me, peering into my soul with her discerning blue eyes. My son just flopped on top of me, snuggling into my neck.

I tried to turn my head to see the clock. I didn't know how much time had passed.

My thoughts poured in....

What time is it?

How much longer until Michael comes home from work?

What the fuck is wrong with me? Oh my god, I can't move my legs. Why can't I move?

Oh shit, I don't want to send my kids to therapy in their future because they remember feeling powerless when their mom fainted in the kitchen.

What a shitty mom I am.

Oh shit... shit... shit.... How can I reframe this and make it less scary?

Common Paden, be the fun mom. They can't know anything is wrong.

"Mommy's just tired. Let's play a game called laying on the floor" I was relieved I could speak, but the words landed flatly. There was nothing fun about this. Even my one-year old knew that.

My eyes welled up with tears.

You can't let them see you like a basket case.

I said, "Come give mama a hug." They both complied. Then Kennedy picked up my purse and started rummaging around. "Where's Meena Mom?" *Shit.* I'd forgotten her favorite Beanie Baby toy. It must've been at the office.

I lay there, silently choking back tears, as both kids clung to me. After what felt like an hour, I managed to roll over and army crawl myself to the living room. I got my daughter to hand me the remote control, and I did what had become all-too-normal during the pandemic ... I turned on cartoons.

The kids instantly got into their couch positions, and their faces went into the blank TV- watching expressions that made them look like they were being programmed. I managed to get myself back to the kitchen.

Do you think this is what a GOOD mom would do?

Is this the best you can come up with? MORE cartoons? That's your answer?

Shut up, I told Bitchy Brittany.

Why didn't you see this coming?

I remembered all the times I flippantly joked to people that the pandemic was just an experiment called, "How much can one woman handle before she breaks?"

Well, fuck. I guess I found out.

But I knew the truth. This hadn't come out of nowhere. There had been red flags for MONTHS. I'd changed my skin care line three times trying to stop the oil pockets forming on my forehead. I'd been getting my period every ten days for the last six months. Maybe the dizziness was from blood loss? I couldn't remember basic things. Not in a mom-brain way, but in a pea soup,fog-brain kind of way. I felt stupid 24/7. Kind of like that time in 8th grade when I literally couldn't remember how to spell the word THIS after taking the summer off of school. I'd been gaining weight around my stomach, and I was super self-conscious that the "gym owner" had a muffin top. But I just pushed down any concerns I had. Trying to ignore them. There wasn't time. I wasn't the priority.

How could I begin to explain this to Michael? What if he took it personally, like the life we'd built together wasn't good enough for me, or was pushing me to the point where I'd rather be alone in an office than at home?

It's not like I could ever tell my stay-at-home mom friends what just happened. They'd just shoot me a pitying look that says, "I'm so sorry you think growing a business is more important than growing humans." Ugh, I couldn't take that. I pictured all the stay-at-home moms making perfect Pinterest dinners for their families while their 4-year-olds read books to the rest of the kids... while mine watched their mom faint in the kitchen. My own mother would have been horrified if she saw this. Even my working mom friends, who normally could relate and laugh with me at all my stories of mom guilt and trying to balance it all, wouldn't be laughing now. They'd probably think I'd lost it.

In that moment, I felt so alone, and my inner chatter wouldn't relent. This time it was Pleasing Prudence.

Did you really think you could do it ALL?

Save the company?

Keep everyone employed while your business is shuttered?

Navigate a freaking pandemic?

See no friends and have no support?

Then Bitchy Brittany chimed in.

So much for female empowerment.

Your feminism is driving you insane.

You're a joke.

You're a failure.

"No I'm not," I tried to put my inner critics in their place....

I searched for the right word. "I'm scared." *Fuck.* That felt more true than anything else. "I'm scared." I repeated out loud to myself. And that's when the tears came. I couldn't stop them.

"Body…. listen to me. I need you. You can't quit on me. I can't do this without you. Please."

Please.

How desperate.

How pathetic.

How did you let it get to this point?

And with no one to pretend for… I just let myself cry out all the stress I'd been harboring inside me for the last seven months.

THE PROBLEM WITH SELF HELP

To date, this was my lowest point, topping even my 2010 heart smash. That time I cried myself to sleep for weeks, realizing I'd spent years in a codependent, toxic relationship I thought was about love, but was really about trying to change and fix someone so you would feel loved back. That was shitty. But this was worse. Because this time I felt actually helpless and scared. and being helpless and scared made me angry. I wish I could tell you the pandemic is what pushed me to this edge. It certainly provided the backdrop for this stage 5 meltdown. But the truth is, I had a history of dealing with drama and stress.

I mean, I gave myself an ulcer at age 23 from drinking so much coffee on an empty stomach and proudly grinding out 100-hour work weeks. Hustle was like a badge of honor. It was what so many had taught me was the main ingredient in the recipe for retiring at age 50.

And as an Enneagram Three, that was all I wanted to be: a success.

I did NOT want to be someone who couldn't get off the damn floor of their kitchen in the middle of the day in front of my kids.

THAT woman was not me. I had spent years thinking I was inspirational, a role model for female leaders and entrepreneurs, someone who could have it all and help other women to believe they also could have it.

So, I followed the breadcrumbs of every inspirational role model of mine, and as far as I could see, I had done everything right. I bought the Carol Dweck victim mindset book. I'd devoured Byron Katie's work and even had her damn app on my phone to practice "doing the work" on the fly. I'd read the female empowerment books, feeling like Glennon Doyle and even Brene Brown had written books for me. I mean of course I was a GDC (God Damned Cheetah). I spent hours in therapy. I'd even gone to a Finding the Love You Want retreat with Michael back when he didn't like me as his boss, and I wasn't sure we could continue to work together and be happily married. I was the retreat girl who would immerse myself in these "transformational experiences" put on by Tony Robbins or Brendon Burchard. I had been part of exclusive 7- and 8-figure CEO masterminds. I invested in coaches, experts and coaching programs to become the best version of myself. I was asked to speak and train Fortune 500 companies on things like, "How to Beat Burnout" or "How to Set Boundaries in Your Life." And I even had my own damned podcast called "Paden's Pep Talks".

And THAT's what made me so fucking angry.

I'd done all the right things. I'd been the good student. I'd easily invested $100k in self-help and thousands of hours absorbing information and what had it got me? A front-row seat of the view of the kitchen ceiling, hiding tears of panic from my kids.

In the business world that would be a shitty return on investment. It sure felt like one. It's one thing to KNOW things, but it's another to figure out how to integrate it. Ugh, my life felt like the leaning tower of Pisa.

chapter 2
SOUL ADVENTURE

"This is a lot of information to process on a Tuesday morning"
- David Rose, *Schitt's Creek*

I was basically dared to go to Sedona by a mentor I admired and wanted to impress. That's what got me to Sedona. Allyson Byrd came into my life in the middle of the pandemic. A bold, victorious voice on a podcast, as I drove home from Trader Joe's, no kids in the car. My definition of self-care that day. Running errands alone, listening to bits and pieces of a podcast as I drove around. I remember being so drawn to Allyson because every single word that dropped into my earbuds was absolute gold. Like #goals for someone like me who journaled daily, "I am a sought after motivational speaker."

I was so transfixed, I remember thinking, "How do I get this woman's voice in my head to dropkick Bitchy Brittany and Pleasing Prudence the hell out and infuse me with daily doses of genuine soul and inspiration?"

And as if she heard me, the next line that came out of her mouth was, "When the student is ready the teacher will appear." Then she pitched her intimate mastermind called Soul Sessions.

I had to be there.

Twenty-four hours later I booked a speaking event that covered the investment needed, and I grabbed one of the last spots. But here's the thing about powerful, wise and bold women, they expect you to rise up in your power, and no one does that better than Allyson Byrd.

Cut to me feeling intimidated and inspired on day one. And, of course, being an Enneagram three, an empath and someone who grew up performing for love and acceptance, I wanted to please her. So when I started talking in circles about feeling stuck in my life and feeling frustrated that I didn't feel connected to my intuition or life purpose, and reeking of privilege, I got called out.

She interrupted me and calmly said, "Stop waiting for the universe to show up and delight you." She pregnant-paused to let me absorb the message, then continued with one of the most profound pieces of advice I'd ever been given, "Paden, you have to show up for your own rescue as much as you are asking for it. If you want something extreme from the universe, get extreme with the universe."

I nodded as if I had the faintest clue what "getting extreme with the Universe" meant. Was it a naked dance out in a forest while micro-dosing mushrooms? Hell if I knew. But thank God she followed up her wisdom with a literal action item.

"Girl, you need to get yourself to Sedona on a Soul adventure. Email me after class and I'll give you my Angel Guide Rick's number. Call him. Go for a full week."

Some things in life just hit you in your heart as divine direction. They are so aligned for you that you feel compelled to follow them with every fiber in your body.

And I felt that kind of alignment then. It was the next step. The gut instinct I thought was mute, spoke up and said, "Go!"

I'd paid for a mastermind to be directed to an almost 5-figure soul adventure week in the high desert of Arizona ... during a pandemic we still had to survive.

But I knew I had to. The next day I texted Angel Guide Rick, "Hi, I'm a friend of Allyson's, and she's recommended that I speak to you about designing my soul adventure." It was a small action, but as a professional "doer," it felt good to do something to move myself forward.

WHAT THE HELL IS AN ANGEL GUIDE?

I have a gift for making decisions on 40% of the information most people need to feel confident. So when my phone buzzed to let me know I had a call with Angel Guide Rick in ten minutes, I laughed at myself.

What in the actual hell is an angel guide? Like is this someone who is an angel in human form and actually has the balls to tell people that? Was it someone who preferred spending time in the fields with beings of the universe? Was this person a shaman? Or a holy person? I was so curious about this title, I couldn't wait to talk to Angel Guide Rick.

Turns out he is a masterful life coach, hypnotherapist, and intuitive empath who, in five minutes of asking me to tell him about myself, had me sobbing like a baby and sharing all my inner wounds. Turns out Angel Guide Rick is a big-hearted man who felt to me like someone who could stitch your soul back together while you slept, and you'd wake up the best version of yourself.

After patiently listening to me trying to be as raw and honest as I knew how to be and act more evolved than I really am for forty-five minutes, he summarized his diagnosis effortlessly, "So it sounds like, Paden, you're a high achiever whose soul is crying out for purpose, and you're stuck because you have deep childhood wounds and pain around religion that have caused you to silence your inner intuition, and you don't know how to trust yourself to create a fulfilling life of passion."

Speechless. He nailed it. So much so that I cringed inside with how broken I looked. I hate when my cracks show. He listed out a five-day itinerary for me with the most woo woo, fluffy session names I'd ever heard.

Seriously you can't make this stuff up. He had me down for:

- Radiant Heart Healing
- Letting Go Ritual On the Land
- Inner Journey with Breath and Sound
- Sand Play for the Soul
- Becoming the Goddess Within
- And half a dozen other sessions with equally entertaining titles.

"How does that sound?" he asked.

I wanted to say, "So batshit crazy my grandma would be rolling in her grave thinking about me exploring this." But like all good girls, I found more appropriate words. "I have no idea what any of that means, but I'm here for the adventure and will try to show up open minded." Regardless of how uncomfortable I was saying phrases like Angel Guide, becoming a goddess, or rituals on the land, I still felt in my gut that this would be so healing for me. Allyson's words rang in my ear, "It's a decade of therapy. I've sent eight of my friends there and each one of us had different itineraries. Just trust the process."

So I did. In my mind I was going to Sedona. The next hurdle was getting my husband on board. This soul adventure would be impossible without his support because following my intuition meant leaving him to run our two businesses and manage two little kids, three nannies, and continue sleep training our son for an entire week. It was a big ask. And as much as I believed I was destined to go, I felt so much guilt asking him to support me in this. It took me days to approach the conversation.

I finally did after Angel Guide Rick texted me that he had one opening left in fall of 2020, and if I didn't book that day, his next opening was in icy cold January. I thought about that Ritual On the Land session during high desert winter and knew I had to go right away.

I went right over to Michael and told him I wanted to go on a Soul Adventure right in the middle of a pandemic that had devastated our finances and go dark as the CEO of the company right before we were likely to be mandated to train outdoors in winter.

Damn I love my husband. He quickly said, "Go for it! You need this trip. I'll do whatever I can to support you, but how do you want to pay for it?" Thankfully, in my days of procrastinating this conversation, I'd planned for my answer to this. I'd already booked two more speaking engagements and had the money to do it.

SOBBING INTO MY MASK AT THE SUPERMARKET

I was crying.

Right there in WholeFoods.

Crying.

Oh, and sniffling. It sounded like I had a snotty cold that I was doing a piss poor job covering up.

An older woman glowered at me over her mask. I could almost read her mind as she passed, "How dare she show up in public sick, during a freaking pandemic!"

But I paid her no mind, the only thought I had in my head was how thankful I was that I had a mask to cover 60% of my face and keep this embarrassing mini-meltdown to myself. I was literally holding Alfredo sauce and choking back tears, trying to regain composure. I couldn't remember the last time I'd been on a shopping trip solo for the sole purpose of choosing food only I would consume and enjoy. For the last decade, shopping trips have only grown more complicated, as I tried to remember and plan for everyone's preferences. Kennedy only likes plant protein. Jackson doesn't like to eat but will sometimes choke down a hot dog or piece of beef jerky. Michael doesn't like fish. I don't like shrimp or sausage. And that's just protein. But this time I was solo and could eat whatever the hell I wanted. You'd think that would have been a blissful experience, but I felt like I was on a first date and had no idea what to say or what to expect. I was overwhelmed—plain and simple.

After wandering through countless aisles for a good half an hour, I started to cry. I didn't know what I wanted. I didn't really know my preferences or even favorite items.

How are you 34 years old and you can't even shop for yourself? How pathetic.

I hadn't asked myself, "Paden, what do you want?" in a VERY long time. What I'd wanted for the last four years had been for my kids to eat and my husband to thank me for a yummy dinner. MY wants were the furthest thing from my mind. Trying to be "selfless" had apparently worked. I was without any sense of self, literally melting down in public trying to remember ANYTHING I liked. Alfredo sauce. It used to be my childhood favorite sauce for ravioli. Okay, good! That's a start.

I took a breath and went through the supermarket like Marie Kondo, only putting into my basket what gave me a spark of joy. I walked out of the store with the most random assortment of foods and certainly overbought.

I even snuck in a bottle of rosé, despite the instructions from Sedona Soul Adventure NOT to drink or use recreational drugs. If there was ONE thing I knew that I liked in this world, it was rosé, but it had to be from Provence, France. My stomach couldn't take American wine laced with chemicals from Round Up. Rosé had got me through sleep training not once, but twice. She was coming with me.

I inhaled. I had just melted down in a grocery store because I didn't know what the hell I liked to eat. Did that really just happen? I hadn't even started my soul adventure. I was a wreck. Heaven only knew what the rest of the trip would be like.

RED ROCKS DRIVE AND STEVIE NICKS

It was day one of my five-day soul adventure, andvI got into my rental car, Googled the address of my first appointment, and damn it, 25-minute drive. I did the quick math. Yep, I'd be 10 minutes late. This time I was worried about what Angel Guide Rick would think of me. Like on a scale from 1 to 10, how much MORE of a basket case, in need of spiritual healing, would I be if I was 10 minutes late? I tried to stop stress-shaming myself on the drive. I was 20 minutes out, and there was nothing I could do about it. I turned out of the resort parking lot and felt like I'd walked right into an incredible painting. Wow. Just wow. The majesty of the red rocks of Sedona melted my stress away. I was in genuine awe. I will forever associate "Gypsy" by Stevie Nicks with falling in love with Sedona because at that moment I heard the lyrics:

To the gypsy
That remains
Her face says freedom
With a little fear
I have no fear
Have only love
And if I was a child
And the child was enough
Enough for me to love
Enough to love

Ahh … this place felt sacred and like home to me. I hadn't even been to a session, and I already felt Sedona was home.

INNER CHILD WORK WITH TALL WHITE MAN NAMED SEQUOIA

When you hear the name Sequoia, you think medicine man or shaman. You don't think tall skinny white dude in his 50s whose deep, slow voice instantly makes you feel like you are talking to Sam Elliott. But then again, my name was Paden. I mean, a Gaelic surname doesn't exactly scream blond American girl. I'd bet I'm not what people expect.

I parked my car and got out to meet my first … therapist? I don't even know. I mean I never even asked what types of experts I'd be meeting with! Do they even have credentials? The number of questions I didn't think to ask before going on this trip was starting to stack up. We had three hours to hike. Me alone with Sequoia, and I didn't even have pepper spray. Fuck.

We started off making small talk with me falling into my networking schtick of finding small insignificant details to strike up a friendship. But small talk wasn't his thing. I found out what was quickly: Digging into childhood memories, learning about my parents, my husband, and life experiences.

The tables turned, and his curiosity was leading me, not the other way around.

I obliged, chattering on and on, and he listened. Before I knew it, he'd moved on from outlining the strengths and weaknesses of my parents, to how my husband and I fit into that and how 99% of my painful life experiences stemmed from inner child wounds. Which we all have.

It wasn't my first rodeo with inner child work. It's the kind of phrase you drop into conversations casually so people know "you know how to do the work." It's like an IG reel, "Tell me you do therapy without telling me you do therapy." Inner child work. Bam! IFYKYK. Okay, so I equate inner child work to therapy because during the very first therapy session I ever walked into, the therapist had me imagine myself as a little girl and recognize how much I wanted to protect her, and of course, how my desire to protect myself pushed people I loved away, reinforcing my abandonment fears.

Oh man. Here we go again.

He handed me a list of all the deepest wounds people have and asked me to read them out loud and tune into the one that I had a visceral response to.

I read:

I am not perfect

I am not good

No one cares about me

I am not good enough

Woah ... I could barely speak that one out loud. My throat choked and my stomach twisted.

I am not good enough.

Since I could remember, I've poured time, attention, and so much stinking effort into being seen as GOOD ENOUGH. He asked me to write down all the mean things I tell myself when I don't think I'm good enough. I made the list. And damn my inner mean girl was landing some punches:

Paden, you are unlovable

You are too strong for people

You will end up alone

No one will love you as you are

No one understands you

You don't matter

You aren't special enough

You're forgettable

You're a failure

I felt heavy and nauseous. I hoped that was the extent of the session. I should have known better.

He then asked me to visualize my inner child. I pictured my school picture at age 6. So innocent, with bangs, long hair and the sweetest smile. Then he asked me to read the list of all the harmful lies to her.

Out loud.

Nope. Hard pass. I said I couldn't do that.

"Why?" he asked.

It was too mean. No one should say things like that to a child. He sat there in silence. My mind was racing...

... doesn't he know I've been verbally abused?

... how the hell is verbally abusing my inner child helpful?

And that's when it hit me. He knew something I hadn't ever admitted, I'd been internally abusing myself for decades. In the shadows of my inner world, I was my own abuser. Both the villain and the victim of abuse. And totally unaware . . . until that moment.

By asking me to do it out loud, he was forcing my mean girl out of the closet and making me bring into the light the internal abuse I'd been unleashing on myself for decades.

Damn. I still didn't want to do it. I felt like if I opened my mouth, I'd start sobbing.

I asked in a quiet voice, "Am I cheating myself of the bigger lesson here if I don't do it?"

"Yep." There it was, that Sam Elliott one-word answer.

I took a deep breath. *Be brave, Paden.* You didn't come all the way out here to NOT complete the exercises.

"Okay."

I picked up the paper and visualized that little girl and did one of the hardest emotional things I've ever had to do. I spoke out loud all the horrible things I'd normalized telling myself when I thought no one was listening. When I finished, I laid down the paper and stared off into the space before us. I was emotionally spent. He asked me to tell him what my inner child looked like. Really dude? The abuser has to make eye contact with the abused? I felt like someone who'd whipped a child with a belt and then looked to see how the child reacted. In my mind's eye, my seven-year-old self looked up to me with big eyes filled with tears and the sweetest expression on her face, an expression of deep compassion for me, clearly seeing the pain I'd caused my adult self. Then she hugged me. No joke. It was so vivid to me and was playing out like a movie.

I instantly knew two things.

1. She saw my pain. She saw my prison of performance. The prison I'd lived in, believing I wasn't good enough. And she knew it was self-imposed.
2. She was an empath. So deeply could she feel my pain that she wanted to help me, and she hugged me with all her heart.

I lost it and cried tears that can only beckon healing, covering my face in my hands and rocking back and forth feeling how deep the pain had penetrated my identity. Sequoia then kindly walked me through that horrible list of lies and made me combat each lie with at least one truth that proved the lie was false. It was so much harder to come up with this list, but I finally managed the following:

- Paden, you are thoughtful, playful, and empowering, and your family loves you.
- Your strength is exactly what draws the right people to you.
- You are always surrounded by wonderful people who value you.
- The more you show up as yourself, the more people love you.
- Your inner child understands you. Lean into that.
- You're a success. You built your business to be in the top performing fitness facilities in the country. When you hit 7-figures, that placed you in the top 2% of female CEOs.

You're a breadwinner in your house. You're always investing in yourself and turning it around to help others succeed too.

• You are special. You matter to Kennedy, Jackson, and Michael.

Then he made me read this list out loud and my heart soared. It felt more true than the list of lies. Recognizing that, my prison felt like it vanished. I remember walking away from that first session thinking, "Well, session one was worth the entire trip!" And it was only the first session. I went to the hotel and poured myself a well-deserved glass of rosé.

chapter 3
THE NOT-SO-RADIANT HEART

"If that's a joke, I love it. If not, can't wait to unpack that with you later."
- Ted Lasso

When Angel Guide Rick first sent me the itinerary for all the sessions it would take to give me a true soul adventure, the one that sounded strangest was this "Radiant Heart Healing" session, with none other than Cher. (I swear the names of these healers kill me.)

I mean if anyone could restore a youthful vibrancy to my heart, it'd be a woman named Cher, but what's with this term "healing?" Healing what? And what's going to happen for the full 90 minutes? Like what are these therapists actually trained to do to allow them to heal people?

Paden, you're on an adventure. You're not in an academic setting where you have to know everything first. Like most adventures, you have to embrace how little you know and just dive into the experience.

That's what I was trying to do, I reminded myself. I walked into the Radiant Heart Healing session partly curious and still trying to push down my inner skeptic, but Cher looked like a sweet grandmother. Cher had champagne-colored hair that looked like it had sat in hot curlers earlier that day. She had piercing blue eyes, a graceful smile, and wore the colorful silk kimono of an artist. She felt wise, and I felt more comfortable.

We started off talking about my life. Once again I was asked, "So tell me about yourself, Paden."

I flashed back to being in senior year in college and being asked what career I was going to pursue. It always got a deer-in-the-headlights reaction from me. So much pressure built up in a question. I didn't know where to start, so I pretended this was an online dating profile, throwing a bunch of fun facts up on a wall to try to see what sticks.

Then she started to tell me a lot about her journey. She started as a scientist, then realized she was more interested in psychology, so she became a therapist, somehow got a PhD along the way, and then realized that healing people through therapy wasn't as effective as energy healing. So she left her job, her business, her clients and moved to the spiritual community of Sedona and became a healer. There was that word again. I mean this lady was smart, like super smart, and in a way where she knew it but had let go of the ego around her knowledge.

She had me lay down on a massage table, and I thought, "Oh, she's a massage therapist!"

We had massage therapists at our fitness center. I felt more comfortable. The comfort lasted exactly three seconds. "Do I undress?" I asked naively.

"Oh no, this isn't a massage. It's energy healing," she said. Wow, this just got even weirder. Now it's called energy healing. WTF is energy healing?

She smiled. Then she pulled out a crystal on a long chain out from the pocket of her pastel-colored robe. My eyes bulged out of my head.

What you should know about me is that I have always been the kind of patient who has to know everything a doctor is doing to me because I like to think I'm smart enough to follow along, and I'm always trying to learn new things. Once I had a dentist talk me through, play by play, how he extracted all my wisdom teeth while I was still conscious because at the time I couldn't afford anesthesia.

So I quickly asked, "What is that?" I honestly didn't know.

I was a mix of curiosity and skepticism. Was this magic? Was 'energy healing' spiritual jargon for magic?

In a blink, Cher had just morphed from a super smart, ambitious scholar into a slightly sketchy witch. The first one I'd ever met. She said she was going to balance my chakras. What are chakras? I asked, somewhat alarmed to have plural body parts I didn't know the names for. "Chakras are energy centers in your body's energy field. You have seven main chakras that are in specific locations on your body, starting from your pelvis up to the crown of your head. Each one is closely connected to specific emotions, body parts, and regulate various bodily functions."

Well, I had to admit that was fascinating. I instantly flashed back to that time I tried acupuncture and saw a rainbow banner with different colors on it going from red, to orange, all the way to purple. I think that's what she was describing to me.

As she described chakras, she held her crystal over my pelvic floor region .. nly it wasn't standing still; it was swinging in a circle. I kept my eye sharply focused on her hand. I wasn't stupid. She had to be moving her hand to make that crystal swing. It wasn't swinging on its own. But I couldn't for the life of me detect movement in her hand!

I asked her what was making the crystal move?

She said the pendulum was connected to her energy, and she was connected energetically to universal consciousness, or God, so she could use it to ask yes or no questions, or she could use it to represent the energy field of each chakra, and the larger the circle, the more open the energy was, which is what she wanted to see.

Yep, this was as hippie-dippie as I had ever ventured. All I got from that description was that circles are good, and so far, mine were all open and large circles, which somehow made me feel good about myself. Like, I wanted to take credit for these robust and open chakras, something I'd only just learned existed.

I watched as she moved her pendulum up to my belly button, then my sternum. Each time the circle grew larger, and I felt prouder of myself somehow. But then she got above my heart, and the circle stopped and then reversed directions. I frowned, and instantly started to look at her hand. Was this lady a con? The pendulum had literally switched directions … her hand barely showed a tremor.

"Okay, what does THAT mean?" I asked, concerned.

"It shows me that you give love easily, but you don't know how to receive love."

WOAH! Dead accurate. In a, oh -shit-I-feel-really-awkward-and-uncomfortable-hearing-that-from-you kind of way. I thought back to all the times I heard compliments, and I brushed them off. All the times I complained about not feeling loved and the frustrated feeling I'd known of showering people around me with love but still operating at a deficit inside. What if I'd actually been blocking love from entering? What if it wasn't true that I wasn't loveable? What if I wasn't letting love in?

Holy shit. That felt really true. I saw in my mind the faces of people I've wanted love from. There were so many times I didn't feel loved. Had they been trying to show me love, and I just couldn't receive it? That felt more true than them never loving me.

This flipped the script on so many relationships I'd felt victimized by. Again, I wasn't the victim. Yesterday I learned I was the abuser of my inner child. Today I learned I was the one blocking myself from feeling loved, and I *paid* for this?

I paused my hyper analyzing at this point, guessing Cher could also read my mind, which I didn't like thinking about. I still didn't know how that damn crystal pendulum had revealed this about me, but I had to admit it did feel pretty magical and powerful—n a good way.

She checked the rest of the chakras and then confirmed to me that every other chakra was open.

Okay. Now what?

"We need to heal your heart chakra through my radiant heart healing process."

I felt empowered, like we identified a specific issue, and I wanted it to heal. So I lay down and she told me she'd connect to spirit and then channel the energy of the universe directly into my heart and that she'd walk me through various visualizations to help my heart soften and open again.

I just went with it. I felt warmth start to tingle from the top of my head. She asked me if I could feel the energy and where? I said it was a warm yellow glow coming in from my crown.

"Oh good," she said. "You can already see color."

What does that mean, I wondered, but I tried to stay in the visualization because no matter how she was healing me, I wanted to be healed. I wanted to feel love being given to me.

Then she said she's guiding the energy to my heart space. I could feel the warmth spread into my head, down my throat, and into my heart. My skin, at this point, has goosebumps. I couldn't deny that something was definitely happening.

She had me visualize my heart as a tiny rose bud that hadn't bloomed. She had me visualize it blooming and opening. She sent more energy. I pictured the yellow sparkly light coaxing the pedals to open. Then I felt a flow of energy fill my chest. I felt light, like my body was glowing from inside but also like I may float off of this table. It was a powerful session.

Afterwards, Cher told me I reminded her of herself. She also said, "Paden, you know you're a healer too,' right?"

I didn't know anything of the sort. What I did know was that I could NOT possibly feel more resistance to a word than I do to the word 'healer,' even after experiencing that.

I raised my eyebrows in disbelief. She smiled, pulled out her pendulum, told me forward and back meant "yes" and side-to-side meant "no," Then she asked how many spirit guides and angels were surrounding me right now.

"10?" The pendulum spun "yes."

She smiled and kept increasing the count.

"20?" Still "yes."

"30?" And she went on until "150," and the pendulum spun "yes." "160?" It changed directions.

"You see," she said, "only gifted healers have more than 100 angels surrounding them. You are special. You have all the Claires. You are one of us."

I smiled, consciously trying to "receive" the love she was sending. Wondering if just by setting an intention to receive and be open, it could work.

But in truth, I didn't identify as a healer. Yet, I was impressed with her knowledge, and of course, I loved hearing that I was somehow special. But I still was not resonating with the word healer at all. This was all a bit much for me.

I mean, the week before I was crunching numbers on how many horse-stall mats we need to fill 4,000 square feet of the outdoor facility we have to build next week to keep up with indoor fitness restrictions. Next thing I know I'm laying underneath a witchy healer with a dancing pendulum being told I'm just like her. (You can't make this stuff up.)

I drove back to where I was staying, made myself alfredo pasta, and got a text that my daughter was missing me and asking if I would call her. My stomach twisted. Was it okay to take this time for myself? Was I ditching the kids for my own healing, and was that going to wind Kennedy up and drop kick her ass into therapy in a decade? Without a doubt, I'm cracking my heart wide open and allowing for some much needed, yet painful, healing. But there was no doubt it was coming at a cost. I'd known it would be really hard to be away from my littles for a whole week;hat's why I'd wrapped up a new present for them to open for every day I was gone. Maybe that would give them something to look forward to and not dwell on how much I knew they'd miss me. I was like their security blanket in human form. I tried to FaceTime them during dinner. My four-year-old liked it and chattered happily about picking an apple off the neighbors' tree. She held it up proudly to show me. "I'm waiting to eat it until you come home Mommy." I tried to smile in a believable way, but I felt a deep sense of longing to hold her and give her a big kiss on that cute forehead. Then I tried to say hi to Jackson. At 14 months old, he had no idea what was going on. "Mama?" He tried to touch my face through the screen of Michael's iPhone. Then he started whining, and that quickly progressed to tears. Michael looked overwhelmed, "I don't think this is helping. Can I talk to you later?"

"Sure," I said, feeling his pain with handling bedtime solo.

Why couldn't I have figured this shit out before kids?! I mean, I was totally screwed up back then. *Because, stupid, you didn't have the money for therapy.* You couldn't even pay for a sinus lift and traded out for it.

You were so broke in your 20s.

True, but what I wouldn't give to go back to my life pre-kids to go on a soul adventure and take a week to dive deep and spare myself the struggle of trying to save two businesses during a pandemic and having two kids under four AND figuring out all my emotional shit. WTF had I been thinking?

You didn't think. You just knew you had to go. Something deep inside of you was pulling that.

Don't question that. Just be proud that you listened.

The truth is there is never a good time for this kind of work. You're walking through the valley of your own shadow, and this shit is hard. Most of us spend decades running from the reality that growth is like a tree, we can only grow as tall as we're willing to reach our roots deep into our darkness.

I wanted to pour another glass of rosé. Shoot! I hadn't pumped yet. I grabbed my Willow breast pumps. Dammit, of course I'd only remembered to bring one. Now it would take twice as long to pump. I mean, there I was every freaking night pumping so my rock hard nursing boobs didn't explode during a healing session. This was a very real scenario by day three.

I felt overwhelmed. I was processing so much deep pain, while missing my family and feeling the weight of mom guilt that was so hard to shake. This felt like a form of torture. But deep down I had a peaceful sense I was where I needed to be. I was reminded in my heart that growth comes from discomfort.

I continued to meet more "healers" the next couple days, and there were more breakthroughs, and more reminding me "you're one of us." One lady opened her door, saw me, and blurts out, "Holy shit, it's like looking at myself 20 years ago!"

Meanwhile, my phone remained free of notifications. It was spooky. No texts. No emergencies. Everyone was giving me space.

Life is just a trip. Last week I was getting texts around the clock from everyone from nannies, to clients, to team members, and just keeping up with my to do list was overwhelming.

PSYCHIC SHOPS AND CHEATING ON JESUS

Angel Guide Rick had made me a lovely print out map of Sedona and had circled all the spots I needed to travel to meet with each healer. He also took the liberty of circling some 'cannot miss' spots while I was there.

I hate missing the "can't miss" spots, but the last one was The Center for the New Age. I was driving back to my Airbnb for my last night before flying home, turned down the fork in the road, and BAM! There it was literally GLOWING in the dark, thanks to a well-placed light bulb. It had a large weird-ass wall mural of religious figures holding hands circling the world. It seemed to be beckoning me to explore. *Should I go? It would be a shame to miss out on something that's supposed to be cool.*

Nope. Pleasing Prudence was right in my ear. *You may as well be cheating on Jesus if you set foot in there.*

Sorry Pleasing Prudence, we're going to have to test how unconditional Jesus' love is on this one.

I parked and walked in trying to act like it was very normal for me to be there, but inside I felt about as awkward and nervous as I did when I walked into Planned Parenthood to get birth control in college.

There were floor-to-ceiling crystals. I'd been to plenty of crystal shops growing up, but this was different. Instantaneously the center of my forehead started throbbing and pressure was building behind my eyes. In less than 30 seconds, I had a full-blown headache, but I'd already popped the cherry and was in the gift shop, so I pretended to know what the hell I was looking at, some stone with a name like Labrador.

Weird. The woman behind the counter gave off the witchy vibe Pleasing Prudence had been afraid of, peering at me. I stared back trying to figure out if she was actually casting a spell. "You have such a lovely purple aura, my dear," she said with a pleasant smile.

Is that a compliment? I couldn't tell. As someone who had only just learned what a chakra was, I made a mental note to Google the word aura when I got into the car. I smiled, as one would who knew they did indeed have the best damn purple glow in town and said, "Thank you," and walked to the other side of the shop.

Okay, I thought to myself, this place is weird. How do I get out? There isn't a quick exit door. I looked and found one, but it turned out to be a back staircase leading up to God only knows what.

The headache had now turned into a full migraine. Why was I still here? There was clearly nothing drawing me to this place. Everything was strange. Everything was creepy.

Then I spotted a familiar face, Byron Katie, right there on the book shelf.

The crystal shop had morphed into a New Age bookstore. One might have assumed the girl who didn't know what a fucking aura was wouldn't know a damn thing about new age books, bBut damn it if every freaking book on the bookshelf wasn't a favorite author of mine, Byron Katie, Deepak Chopra, Dr. Joe Dispenza, Gabby Bernstein, Don Miguel Ruiz …

It literally looked like the bookcase in my bedroom. WTF?

My people. My teachers. The wisest books I've read in the last year, there in the damn psychic store. FML. Don't you think it's ironic that you found your way into the hotbed of your biggest mentors? Why fight it? Just because it doesn't look the way you thought it would. Maybe I am one of them after all.

IDENTITY CRISIS - WHO THE HELL AM I?

As a child I'd felt so much compassion for anyone who was left out, made fun of, or in any way ostracized. I remember when everyone laughed at Wilson because he wore the same hand-knit sweater for a week straight, and I told them to stop laughing and put my arm around him. I remember in 8th grade taking David under my wing because he was clearly flamboyant and unsure about how to show up authentically as a Christian homeschooler. I made sure his style was applauded, his jokes appreciated, and that he had a seat at our table. When I went to summer camp, I'd taken $19.50 with me from my piggy bank. I used it to buy presents for my four siblings who weren't old enough for camp. I wanted them to feel as special as I did.

There were countless times my friends' parents would walk up to my mom with tears in their eyes and thank her for how kind I'd been to their kids during a tough season in their lives. I was sensitive, sure. Kind, absolutely. In tune with the feelings and needs of everyone around me, without a doubt. My heart was my superpower as a child.

But as a 34-year-old, I felt removed from this identity. I felt like my heart had been long ago blocked. I'll spare you a retelling of the people and experiences I lived through that made me no longer feel safe being big hearted and kind. I'd exchanged that sweetness for being hard-minded. It was like armor. Now, I was the blunt, hard-ass who intimidated people in meetings, made decisions, often choosing profit over people, didn't think twice about firing someone or how I made them feel, or hesitate calling back customer service at United Airlines and spew frustration at them until they gave me what I wanted (which, let's be honest, was almost never, but damn, I tried hard.)

The dissonance was never more apparent to me than when I went through five days of seeing healer after healer, all of whom told me the following things:

- You are incredibly intuitive.
- You are a healer, here on earth to help people.
- You remind me of myself when I was your age.
- Your heart is your superpower.

If I'm honest, all this did was propel me into inner conflict.

What? No way. I mean, I do have a weird-ass Gaelic name, which could easily be my claim to healer fame, but I don't think I'm cut from the same cloth as these weirdos.

"But Paden, they are brilliant and changing your life."

I don't want to be like them. I want to be super successful and influential.

"By success, do you mean money and fame, or influence and impact? These healers are creating massive impact one life at a time. Isn't that also success?"

They probably tell everyone they meet that they're a healer to make them feel less weird about the whole thing.

"Maybe, but does it feel true in your body that you're a healer?"

Sort of, but something's missing for me with this healer title. I don't think I'll heal bodies... maybe self-esteem or heartache. I don't know.

"Keep going. Just keep exploring."

I'm the person who is the business coach to bleeding heart entrepreneurs. They would rather work for pennies to bring their gifts to the world. That sounded about as far removed from me as I'd ever heard. But by day five, I couldn't dismiss it because in that week I'd begun the process of softening, or reawakening, and remembering who the fuck I was. It felt true that, like all of us, my natural state is love. I was born into this world a being of pure love, and as I experienced pain or being disconnected, I felt the need to protect, hide, and diminish any part of me that could bring more pain.

This is the great tragedy of humanity. When we come into the world perfect and slowly twist and turn into untrue versions of ourselves, our quest becomes trying to get back to that natural state. Our healing goal, being an epic return to the purity and purpose we entered this world with. It felt clear to me after Sedona that I was somehow meant to be a conduit of compassion and a safe harbor for the broken. Despite my best efforts, maybe I was a healer after all, and that week I'd been reunited with my tribe—a tribe as wise and wild as I've ever known.

chapter 4
TWO HOURS A DAY

"I am very uninterested in that opinion." -
- David Rose, *Schitt's Creek*

THE GERMAN BUDDHA DIAGNOSIS

If there's one thing that hooks me when I meet someone new, it's their tone of voice and word choice. When I met Komala, I felt her compassionate heart and was drawn in by her warm, gentle tones that softened her German accent. It felt like I was in the presence of a beautiful German Buddha. She had a way of sitting fully in her power, while never losing sight of her mission to heal and help. When I learned she was a trained nurse, life coach, and gifted intuitive, it felt too good to be true.

We sat down in her garden, and she gazed peacefully at me before saying, "So, I have you in this group of high achievers, but I also have you as a highly sensitive person, and your body and your nervous system are not set up for how you're living." I sat back, feeling simultaneously alarmed that she read me so quickly and fascinated that she wasn't looking to me to affirm any of her words.

She just kept going. "Your nervous system, genetically, is set up for depth perception and for empathy. It isn't set up to compete with the 80% of the population who are not highly sensitive, and that's what you've been doing. That's the wrong setup. It's not who you are. I need you to hear that because many highly sensitive people in the world don't recognize the gift and suffer from low self-esteem, and when you are a high achiever with low self-esteem, you will push that gas pedal harder and harder. We have some agenda to prove that we are enough or worthy. Whatever it is for you, drop it! Cut it out!"

I was stunned by her gifts of perception. I prided myself on reading people, but she was next level. She'd basically summarized for me the last decade of therapy and even connected some dots I hadn't put together yet … all in the first two minutes of our 90-minute session. I pulled out my phone and hit record. Every word was intentional, every word felt like gold, and she was only just getting started, and I knew Ineeded to relisten to this.

"Your genetic setup is highly sensitive. Life designed you to be sensitive. And what I mean by that is high sensitivity, depth perception, empathy … those are your gifts. When you don't know how to live that, then you suffer from over-stimulation. It's as simple as that." I was still scribbling notes to try to capture how eloquently she just described my gifts to me.

"Paden, how do you know you suffer from over-stimulation?" she asked.

I pictured myself on the kitchen floor and knew the answer. "My body breaks down on me. I have intense energy crashes in the afternoon.

I'm lethargic. I have a foggy brain. I sit at the computer for four hours but get nothing done."

"What's your job? What do you do for a living?"

"I'm the CEO of two companies, a 7-figure fitness and recovery center and a start-up fitness certification and education company."

She nodded. Clearly not surprised to hear that. "As empaths, we have a tendency to really orbit around the people in our environment. Empaths have more mirror neurons firing, which allows us to understand quickly what the environment needs from us, and we adapt. For example, if I were to introduce you to a new culture, I'd give you less than five minutes before you'd be in their dwellings frying up fish with them, laughing. But here's the thing, do you know your default frequency? No. Do you know what your environment expects of you? Yes. Do you find your identity in molding your personality to fit into what the world expects you to be? Yes. Is that your path to happiness? No."

Holy shit!

Is this what intuitive empaths do? She was reading things about me with little-to-no evidence or context, yet seemed to tap into why I felt as I did. This was magical!

She kept talking. "This pressure to mold your personality to fit into what the world expects of you is only amplified by being a wife and a mother. What we do is we orbit around our families Now add in that you're an empath and highly-sensitive … woah! Who are you Paden? I bet you have no idea."

That triggered me for a hot second, but I knew she'd hit the bullseye. Then she went into diagnosis mode. "You need down time. You're in adrenal fatigue right now. Getting your period every ten days, crashing in the afternoon, and not being able to concentrate are all warning signals, like red flags and flashing lights. Paden, you have two opportunities. You either learn this now at age 34, or you ignore it for another two to three years, and then you'll end up with an autoimmune disease that will impact your lifestyle. Either way, you have got to make a change. Choose the rather painless way now, or you'll end up learning it in a more painful way later, but you WILL have to get off what you're doing now. There's no way around this." Then she paused. "What are you going to do about this?"

I felt like I'd been smacked over the head with about fifty quotes I wanted framed in my office. I knew she expected an answer, so I said the first word that popped into my head, "boundaries." Kind of like how in church you could answer "Jesus" and nail it 8 out of 10 times. Same with therapists of any kind ... boundaries seemed to get approving nods more times than not.

"So what are your boundaries?" she asked.

The words came right through me, "I need to take two hours a day for myself." Woah, that felt really right when I said it, also simultaneously horrifying! *Did I really just say that?!?* I hoped she'd disagree with me, but instead she said, "At least! You need *at least* two hours a day." Then she said, "All HSP's must have plenty of downtime to avoid nasty consequences like serious errors, illness, depression, or ruining an important relationship. You need this time to lay down, meditate, and walk. You also need to limit your social life. Even supportive people add to your stimulation load."

We continued to talk for the remainder of the session. She tried to convince me to get a bigger home, so I could have my own meditation room, which sounded lovely, but "buy a new house" was certainly not in the short-term. I could only imagine picking up the phone and telling Michael we should buy a new house, when our businesses had been shuttered by the pandemic, and it was everything I could do to keep my employees paid, and we still were investing $25K into building an outdoor workout space so our members wouldn't put their memberships on hold and sink our ship. Yes, that was NOT going to happen. Even if we HAD the money for a down payment, every dollar was going towards surviving this pandemic. I mean, it was going to be hard enough to sell Michael on me spending two hours a day!

Wow, two whole hours? That's crazy! How did Komala agree with that? Where did I come up with that? I mean, who has time for that?

"You need to get your own space somewhere, a space you can retreat to because you're in a place where you won't even go home because there is too much going on there." The conversation trailed on, and then I realized I wanted to ask about my career and that sense of being "stuck" and wanting more. I blurted out, "I want to be a speaker."

"Yes, I see that for you too, but not until you're about 45 years old. I'm telling you that as a reader."

How does she know when I will pivot my career to being a speaker? That's such a weird thing to say. And why is she calling herself a reader? I could have guessed she learned to read long ago. Why do I get the feeling she's alluding to something else? *Hell, I'm just going to ask.* "When you say you're a reader, what does that mean?"

"Oh, I teach intuition classes. It's one of the traits of the highly-sensitive, to be highly intuitive. I've been working as an intuitive since I was 20-years-old. I teach people how to connect with their intuition; it's part of my gift. So what I'm telling you in this session is to take your lead foot of the gas pedal in your life."

I wasn't totally satisfied with her answer, but I moved on because truthfully, she'd said more wise things in an hour than some people say in a decade.

Her final comment to me, as she walked me back to my car, was, "Your mind thinks it's a Lamborghini, but your body is a Toyota SUV. If you crank that thing at 200 miles per hour down the freeway 24/7, you can basically count the seconds before the motor gives up."

My heart sank. I didn't want to be slow or the one who couldn't pull my own weight. If felt like I was being told to limit my potential, which flared me up inside. I'd always prided myself on being a hard worker, who could hustle with the best of them. Now all I could think about was being compared to a Toyota trying to race with a Lamborghini. Possibly one of the most unflattering comparisons I'd been confronted with. But I tabled that line of thinking for a minute, because Komala hadn't stopped telling me more about myself and what to do to get off the crazy train I'd built and driven.

"Nurture your inner being. This is a really good thing. I would have you restructure your life so it becomes coherent with your body. Anything you add to what you're doing now is going to put you into complete overwhelm."

And that wrapped up the session. I was reeling with so much to process. I said thank you and got into my rental car, which just so happened to be a damn Toyota. Oh, the irony. I drove away with a sense of annoyance for being told I couldn't compete energetically with the rest of the 80% of humans who weren't super sensitive, but I also had a sense of being seen and understood and the strong impression I'd been given a roadmap to charting my physical and soulful success.

I'd come to Sedona to find myself and find a path to happiness, and in this session, she'd given me a prescription for a happy life. Now all I had to do was give myself permission to follow it and the guts to ask Michael to support me on a journey that would no doubt disrupt our lives in the midst of a global pandemic.

chapter 5
WATERBOARDED BY REALITY

"OK. There is only so much that I can do in a day."
- David Rose, *Schitt's Creek*

Driving past my last view of the Red Rocks, one thing was obvious, my life, as I knew it, was not congruent. I was like the girl who had made a list of every quality she wanted in a future partner, only to date the polar opposite. I said I wanted wealth, but I was running my body to the ground. I said I wanted happiness, but I spent a lot of time doing things that left me feeling negative and depleted. I said I wanted growth and to show up as my best self, but not a single minute of any day was dedicated to connecting to my heart or being alone with my thoughts.

I was putting pictures of one thing up on a vision board and lining up activities that may or may not ever lead me to those pictures.

When you realize your life is out of alignment with your vision and dreams, you're on a highway to discomfort. You either ignore it, blame the messenger and continue doing what you know to do, OR you look into the void and realize that everything you want is in the unknown. Which means you need to venture into unknown territory and embrace the discomfort of not knowing if you will find your way. It requires trust, and I decided to trust in a way that felt blind, but at least had marching orders:

Spend two hours a day rediscovering that little kind girl I'd left behind.

Would it surprise you at all to learn that I woke up the next day with a strong optimism about my return home, confident that my new outlook on self and boundaries would be as easy as flipping a switch?

Pre-Sedona burnout achiever. Nope. Flip that switch.

Self-loving, two hour-a-day zen master. Yep. Simple. I could make this happen. It wasn't going to be like every other time I'd gone to a retreat or trip and come back trying to execute 20 new ideas overnight. No, this time felt doable. It was a far cry from my marching orders coming out of Christian summer camp, "Give it to God." As if any of us knew how to do that. No, this time it was practice. Take two hours per day. It was actionable. It was something I could schedule. It was only one thing, and it was a simple thing. But it would require consistency. I was energized and excited by this new prescription for happiness. I had no idea what brought me happiness or what nurturing my soul would actually be like, but after a week of being solo and exploring who I was, I was on my way. That momentum was itself amazing.

Five hours later, I walked through the bright red door of my San Luis Obispo Victorian Era home and both kids ran with open arms shouting "Mama," and I enveloped them in a hug as big as my love for them. I hugged Michael next, exhaling with gratitude for everything he'd taken on to allow me a week alone. He had been happy to do it, but I could tell he was relieved to see me back home, ready to share the responsibilities again.

And there it was, I was back wearing my Mom and Wife hats instantly. Of all the hats I questioned, it was good to be reminded that those felt good to put back on. I was flooded with happiness to see my humans again. Reconnection to people you love is always beautiful. Reentry to the life that landed you on the floor staring up at your kitchen ceiling, however, wasn't.

"Mama!!!!" I woke up to Jackson's 4:40 am screams. Michael patted my shoulder, as if to say, "Welcome back honey. This one's all you."

I had forgotten how early my days started. Since he was born, Jackson's internal alarm clock had been set to 4:40 am, redefining the term "morning person". Fifteen months later, we'd folded and just accepted it. I got out of bed, threw on my hospital bathrobe, and crept into the nursery carefully, in full mom stealth mode. It was sweet to see Jackson's happy face when he recognized me in the dim light of the nursery. He smiled and wiggled with glee. Thrilled to see me and nurse again. My nipples on the other hand weren't so thrilled. The morning snowballed into the typical routine: Michael had to work that Saturday morning, so off he went, and I was back in the saddle solo-parenting. Me juggling two kids, trying to get ready while making breakfast, changing two poopy diapers, while trying to cook the perfect sunny side up eggs, burning the oatmeal on the bottom of the pot, while trying to find the "perfect" YouTube cartoon that both kids would like. I resolved the morning squabbles of the kids playing with each other's toys, as I cooked three separate breakfasts. Three because God forbid the kids eat the same foods, and still I bartered with each one to get them to finish any kind of protein. I finally let them wriggle free of the breakfast table, and I inhaled for the first time in hours.

I reached for my coffee, my sacred morning ritual. It was as if when I held that cup, everything else got muted around me as I sipped it. This is exhausting! It was only 8 am, but man, I had already been non stop for three and a half hours. Yesterday I would have just been waking up now. Ugh!

Welcome back, said Bitchy Brittany. *Not exactly Sedona, is it?*

I hated when Bitchy Brittany said stupid shit. Especially when it made me wish for a different life and feel like a dirtbag as soon as I thought it. The rest of the day pressed on.

I decided to help with some of the domestic parts of keeping the house running. I decided to grocery shop, to get that out of the way. Forty-five minutes, that's how long it takes two kids and me to get dressed to go anywhere. We stood in the long line, in masks, to be let into Trader Joe's. At this point of the pandemic, only 10% capacity was allowed. Fifteen minutes of holding two kids' hands, as they reached for every potted plant in eyesight, trying to remain calm and patient, and wasn't even grocery shopping. Trying to get through a grocery store with two kids under three felt like American Ninja Warrior. I tried to careen through all the obstacles without losing hold of a kid, hitting anyone with my cart, and not forgetting a mission-critical item while being yelled at by both kids at once. I was so over-stimulated, it kicked the zen right out of me.

Within fifteen minutes of being home, I heard the toilet flush and my daughter scream. I followed the billowing toilet paper trail to the scene of the crime. My daughter was screaming as she watched in horror as her brother happily conduced a science experiment, which included flushing Kennedy's favorite troll doll down the toilet.

I blinked, my eyes squinting, trying to will into existence a positive attitude. I wanted so badly to hold onto the feeling of Sedona, but it was fading away with every scream for Mama.

I took a deep breath.

The house was a mess. Not that I was the parent that really noticed that, typically. I'm definitely more of a mess-maker and mess-ignorer in the house, but I felt stifled looking around at all the clutter.

How did we have endless pockets of toys spilling out of corners of the house? I decided we should go for a walk. Maybe getting outside would be the key. It wasn't. Neither was naptime. Neither was family time at the park.

The thing about parenting nowadays is that the stress is rarely condensed into one moment or event of the day; it's spread out and ever present in varying degrees. Some days breakfast is a full on fight, other days it's just a couple negotiations to each take two more bites. Some days grocery store trips are quick and eventless, other times you are literally chasing your toddler through aisles, as people nearly whack your kid in the face with their carts because they don't have a developed toddler radar. Some days everything is hard. Somedays very little is hard. That's precisely why guilt shows up. The inconsistency, yet compounding build up, makes you think you're the one who can't handle it.

Every minute you are "on" as a parent. You are watching every step. You stop what you're doing when it gets too quiet, so you can investigate, anticipating what comes next, and often doing all that while trying to get done some menial tasks that feels like if you don't accomplish it, your life will literally go to shit. It's not that being a Mom is hard every given moment. It's that the hours are long and the demands relentless.

And here it was 5 pm, dinner needed to get started, and I was panicky. I hadn't taken my two hours yet. The ONE thing I promised myself I would do. I felt my throat tighten. What if I couldn't do this? What would happen to everything I'd just discovered in the last week? Would it disappear and go away?

I guess I had hoped finding two hours a day would just naturally happen. Since when did that ever happen? I mean, this was the weekend. I didn't even have work pressure on top of this. I needed to hit pause for a minute. I asked Michael if he'd cook dinner so I could go out for a walk around the block. Thankfully his degree of parenting stress always seems a level or two lower than mine. Juggling dinner and kids doesn't phase him. Is that because I'm so sensitive? Hmm. I hurried out of the house, aware that I really only had twenty minutes. I felt a swell of emotion in my throat and needed to release it, so I put in my earbuds and played the new playlist I'd created while in Sedona called "Paden's Soul Music." The first note of Alanis Morrisette's song "That I Would Be Good" and a giant frog formed in my throat, and my eyes welled up in big slow tears. But it was the .... "That I would be loved even when I'm overwhelmed" line that broke me. There I was crying in front of my house, dy one of being back home. All the ease and calm of Sedona had melted away, and I felt the return of the less desirable anxiety and stress replace them.

No! I didn't just go to Sedona for a week to come back and pick up life the way it was.

I mean, I love my kids and my husband, but the life I'd built was too much.

In 24 hours my central nervous system had me alternating between fight, flight, freeze or fawn to everyone and everything. (But let's be real, my go to was fawning, or people pleasing. The very response I had just learned had disconnected me from myself, my wants, and my desires. The thing I was trying to get back.) I felt panicked inside that I wouldn't be able to change a damn thing about the life that had left me motionless on the kitchen floor. What had Komala warned me about? An autoimmune disease. And Angel Guide Rick had intuitively given it a name: Hashimoto's Disease. Hell no. I had to do something. I had to start taking two hours a day. I mean, I owned a fitness facility, where we helped people create new habits. I knew better than anyone how much resistance we're met with when we move from resolve into action. It's always hard in the beginning, but if you stick with it for a couple weeks, it gets easier.

So what was holding me back?

My inner people pleaser. Fucking Pleasing Prudence. That good girl voice that hates to be the target of hate or conflict.

Paden, don't you think you'll feel guilty coming back from a week all by myself and asking for more time alone? I mean, wasn't it good enough for you that your husband oversaw two businesses and two kids so you could focus only on yourself for an entire week? How many women get to do that? And then if you do take two hours a day, won't you really be telling your kids and husband that for you to be happy, you need to have less time with them? Of course you feel guilty asking for more! You should just be grateful for what you already have and count your blessings.

I didn't want to hurt their feelings. I did have a lot of good things in my life. I was just overwhelmed right now with all the activities, all the demands, and all the busyness of life.

Then Pleasing Prudence said, *If it was going to be good for you, wouldn't you feel better asking for it? Maybe two hours isn't realistic. Maybe settling for something less would be best.* I fought back.

No. I am different. I'm highly sensitive, and that's what's happening to me right now. I never knew before, but right now my central nervous system is overstimulated and overwhelmed because it's just too much going on at once for me. It's the dark side of my gifts. To wish that part of me away would be to miss out on the magic of sensitivity. I'm not going to do that.

I was going to have to learn to live with this sensitivity and stop trying to shove it down or pretend it didn't exist.

Two hours a day. I'd have to try it. If I didn't, what else would I do? I knew the answer to that was more terrifying than trying two hours a day. If I didn't block it off intentionally and instead tried to wait for it to be a good time, it would never come. There is no convenient time to establish a new habit in your life. I knew if I didn't use the last ounce of energy I had from Sedona to push for two hours a day, that it would fade and become a memory. My life would go on. I'd adapt, as usual, to accepting a crazy amount of stress in my life and continue to ignore my needs and count down the days until my next breakdown or diagnosis.

I turned the corner and looked at my little perfect Victorian house in downtown San Luis Obispo. My life looked iconic from the sidewalk, but I still had to walk through the front door and live in it. From afar, it was perfect, but it was far from perfect.

I wasn't going to settle for life being a blur. I didn't want to look back on my kids' childhood and just remember being in a state of resentful survival. Damn, is that why so many freaking parents in their 50's and 60's warn new parents to "enjoy it while they're little. You'll never get it back"? Ugh, I always hated that guilt trip. I didn't want all the work I'd done in the last decade trying to build a great life to end up just feeling like every day is groundhog day.

I didn't want to survive. I wanted to thrive. I wanted to live a full, colorful, incredible life. I wanted to have a vibrant, exciting life, and the only way I knew how to get that was to start doing something so different it would have to shake it up. To do that would be wildly inconvenient, and I was ready for it. I knew in my gut that this two hours a day thing was important.

I had already given myself permission to do it, but I still hadn't brought it up to Michael. I got off that plane thinking there'd be a good time to bring it up this weekend, but there hadn't been a good time. Today was proof of that. I also knew that if I didn't come up with a plan, it would be hard to convince him that it was possible. It was going to be a big ask, and like all the asks I'd ever made in my life, I had to make them ironclad to be assured of success. I had five more minutes until dinner.

How could I fit my two hours in? It couldn't inconvenience Michael, could it? Well at least it couldn't start that way. I didn't want to spend less time with the kids, so that left me working less. Could I do it? Could I steer our brick and mortar fitness business through the pandemic and keep the start up certification business moving towards breaking even in less time? I mean, I had, like all entrepreneurs in the last decade, read the *4 Hour Work Week*. It inspired me, but I didn't do a damn thing about it then. Could I make that happen now? Maybe cut down the time in the office by 10 hours a week? It was worth a shot.

I worked it out on the way back home for dinner. Yes, if I didn't change the nanny schedule at all and just showed up to work at 11 am instead of 9 am, that could work. I knew I had to talk to Michael in the only window of time we could be guaranteed to be both exhausted and uninterrupted—after bedtime.

After the blur that is 5:30 to 7:30 pm in the Hughes' household, Michael walked to the couch with the remote in his hand. I paused, "Hey, can we hold off on watching a show real quick. I want to talk about my big takeaway from Sedona. Are you open to that?" He looked up at me with a look that wasn't completely off board, but would have taken any out provided.

"Please, it's important."

"Sure."

I shared with him that the main thing I really wanted to do was get to know myself better, to actually spend time alone reconnecting to my soul and heart.

He smiled, "Remember when we first met, that you hated to be alone? I think this could be good for you."

I remembered. I couldn't even handle car rides where conversation went silent without feeling like I'd done something to piss him off. *Codependent much?*

Encouraged by his response, I went on, "I came back very clear about something I need to do. I need to schedule a block of time each day to be alone."

"Okay, how much time? Like 30 minutes?"

"More like 2 hours. Actually, exactly two hours."

"Two hours?!? That seems a little lengthy given everything we have on our plates, right?"

"Yes, but it's important. I thought about it on the walk tonight, and if I just do it right after the nanny gets here and before I go to work, I don't think it would be missed."

I mean, I was staring off into oblivion every work day from 2 to 4 pm anyway. No one seemed to notice. I had to imagine if I kicked off my workday with something energizing, I'd be more productive. Hell, I might even get hooked and never go back. But I didn't say that part. Not yet.

"As long as it doesn't hurt the business, I support you trying this out," he said, reminding me of exactly why I love him so much.

"I want to give it three weeks to see if it's as good for me as this healer told me."

"Sounds good. I'm glad you got a lot out of Sedona and glad you're home," he said, as he pulled me close and reached for the remote control. We had a standing appointment with Outlander that evening.

I was relieved. Why had I worked it up to be a difficult conversation? Michael always wanted what was best for me.

And after today, it turned out, I did too.

Monday morning was the same crazy whirlwind of early morning wake ups, closed-eyed coffee sips and the flurry of activity and multi-tasking mayhem.

Then our nanny walked in, and I tried to make the easy exit. To no avail. Both kids clung onto me.

Pleasing Prudence was all over it.

Oh my gosh, those sweet little faces! Paden, maybe you shouldn't be trying to leave your kids so early in the morning. You're in such a rush to do what exactly? Be alone? Don't you think that's a little selfish? Imagine what ten more hours a week with their mom would do for them? Isn't a mother's most important job to raise well-behaved citizens of the world? It's not too late, you could turn back and be a good Mom. You could finally let go of the delusion to have it all. Then they could be happy. After all, isn't being a Mother the most important work of all?

Shut up! I need this. I deserve this, and they deserve a mom who is happy and healthy. That's the best gift I can give them right now.

Damn, that felt good! That was growth right there. Still, I knew on day one of my new habit, I'd be happier if I didn't rip screaming kids from around my neck, so I stuck around, trying to find a fun distraction. Ten minutes later, both kids were happily doing art projects with the nanny, and I managed to slip out the front door undetected.

There it was! My first two-hour block! I had made it happen! I got into the car feeling accomplished and then Bitchy Brittany spoke up.

What exactly are you going to do now? I mean, do you even know what you're going to do to "nurture your soul?"

No, no idea. I hadn't gotten that far. Shit. I'd been so focused just getting my two hours set up so I could have this time. Now that I have it, I didn't even know where to drive. I reached for my Sedona journal. Dang it, it was still in the house, and I couldn't risk going back in and having to make another getaway.

Shoot. I looked at the clock. Dammit, it was already half an hour into my two hours.

Okay, think, Paden. What did they say in Sedona?

Komala said to find time to nurture my soul, doing things I love.

What do I love?

Nada.

Nothingness.

Silence.

Seriously? Bitchy Brittany butted in, soundly super judgmental.

I felt a little like Julia Roberts in Runaway Bride, when she always ordered her eggs the same way each one of her fiancés had ordered it, because she didn't know how she liked her eggs.

Well, there I was in the car, unsure of how I like my happiness cooked. I felt pathetic. Thirty-four years old and not a damn clue of what I liked to do for fun, much less to "restore my soul." So I decided the best idea would be to learn from a random Hollywood script writer from the 90s and do what Julia Roberts did in the movie: cook the eggs in every possible way and do a taste test to find what worked for her.

So I would simply try it all and see what felt best. That felt inspired.

Okay, so on day one I thought I'd dive into meditation. Where could I meditate? Not my office, with loud workout music blaring. Not in the house. I started to see why Komala had encouraged me to get a She Shed for myself. That would be perfect, but I didn't have perfect. I had right now, and that meant my car. I needed to drive to a place where no one would bother me or be bothered by my car.

The good news was that most people worked from home during the pandemic and lots of commercial businesses' parking lots were empty. I decided to drive to one near work. I got there and parked by a basketball court on the side of a massive, new office building that was totally empty. I put the car in park and reached for my phone. YouTube certainly would have some kind of meditation. At this point in my life I'd only known meditation to be a three-minute guided meditation from the app Headspace. Three minutes was my sweet spot. I tried twenty minutes once and fell asleep. But I didn't want to do Headspace. I wanted something that felt more like a journey.

My goal, besides getting healthy and inspired, was to open up my intuition more. I knew I had it. I knew it had moments where it was strong, but I wanted it to be so developed it could be summoned on demand and help me navigate this life better, so I Googled, "best meditation for developing your intuition." Oh God. I mean gosh. The creepiest faces staring with purple eyes peering over crystal balls almost made me rethink my search. But then I saw one that looked normal called, "Developing Your Intuition".

I locked the car doors (because, hello, like any woman in America, I'm hardwired to believe a rapist is around every corner when alone), adjusted the car seat to be more comfortable, put in my airpods, and clicked play.

Breathe in ... Breathe out ...

I started to feel the return of Sedona zen. I was more gratified by this than I thought I would be. It was proof I hadn't been lost in a "summer camp high" but that what I'd connected to was available to me always. I knew, like most things, it would take time and cultivation to draw it out of me and understand what it was and how to use it. I was here. I was ready. I had permission from all stakeholders.

Here we go.

I closed my eyes again ... when...

Oh crap! Are you fucking kidding me?

I had to pee. In classic mom style, zero to sixty.

Annoyed, I hit pause on the YouTube video. I really didn't want to waste my precious time driving to my office to use the bathroom. I glanced around and saw some bushes, but looked skeptically up at the office windows. I couldn't see into them, so literally anyone could be in there. I couldn't pee in the bushes if I thought I'd be in plain sight. Hard pass.

That's when I saw it. My water jar. I chugged the water quickly and did the unthinkable.

I peed into a jar in my car, and that's how it all started.

chapter 6
THE THREE-WEEK TRIAL

"I could not be more at one with nature. I do Coachella every year."
- David Rose, _Schitt's Creek_

I didn't grow up in the era that listened to vinyl records, but I played with one once at a thrift store. I remember the sound of the record playing and how when placing your finger on top of the needle it distorted the song and screwed up the music. I know DJs can make it sound cool, but when I did it, everyone around me cringed.

Imagine doing that, but with words, in front of people you want to impress.

That's what happened for me at a retreat years ago when a mentor of mine was sharing that she was planning her next annual solo trip. She described how she typically takes a couple of weeks a year to be alone and enjoys time with herself. This comment triggered me instantly. I likely raised my left eyebrow, as I'm told I do, in an affronted way listening to her story. As someone who likes to talk out my feelings, I tried to lighten my mood for everyone else and said, "Alone? Seriously, that's my worst nightmare. I can't imagine being alone for even a couple hours, let alone a week or two. Like what would I even do? I'd probably just end up watching shows or reading books, anything to distract myself from feeling alone."

Cue the fffrrrip sound. And then an awkward prolonged silence.

I honestly thought everyone would jump in and agree with me. Like who ACTUALLY likes to be alone like that? I looked around seeking affirmation that I was right in my assumption. But instead Bitchy Brittany jumped in to interpret everyone's non-verbal signals:

They think you're broken because you can't be alone.

Look at their sad looks. They are pitying you for your lack of maturity.

I felt that familiar low-grade anxiety when caught in social settings where all I want to do is fit in and impress, only to realize I'd voiced my opinion and found myself outside the circle of understanding—an outcast. God, I hate that.

My mentor, a wise and intuitive leader of our mastermind, looked at me and said, "I'm sorry you feel like that. I think if you gave it a try, you'd be pleasantly surprised."

"I don't think so, but I'm glad you enjoy it." I was embarrassed that all I'd managed to do was secure their pity. I found a flimsy excuse and extracted myself from the conversation. I'm sharing that story with you now because of its irony and as a trigger warning if you keep reading. It's ironic that several years ago I was so terrified by the concept of taking alone time, and yet here I am writing about it. You've got to love the humor of it all. You can't make this stuff up.

At that time I was "happier" trying to like my non-stop, always productive self than actually digging in and finding out if I could spend time by myself without distraction and enjoy it. But whenever my psyche reminded me of her challenge, I had resorted to the classic cop-outs:

"I don't have time. I have children," or "I have a business."

"Maybe one day when life slows down."

"I don't really need alone time to live my best life. Maybe that's not for me at all."

"I don't want to live a life where I have to retreat from life in order to succeed long-term. Doesn't that just mean you're weak?"

"I feel like I'd just sit there technically alone, but my mind would be in a dead sprint, filling my head with non stop reminders of everything else I should be doing. How is that productive? It just sounds like you're showing up and waiting for a panic attack to build."

But it feels important to share with you that right before going to Sedona, this was my reality. I resisted every single notion of taking time to foster a relationship with myself. It freaked me out for years. I felt judged by the know-it-alls who seemed to have cracked the code to self-love and were there to shove a prescription for a happy life down my throat.

So even though I'd just come back from soul-searching summer camp and hit pause on all the raging demands of my life so I could catch my breath, this three-week test was exactly that. It was a test. A test of will power. A test of whether I could show up for myself and not betray my commitment to my personal well-being. I decided the best way to try it out was almost exactly how a mental health professional would after giving you a prescription.

"Here you go. Take one per day. Don't miss a day for three weeks, and we'll reevaluate how you're doing before we decide to keep going."

I didn't honestly know if I'd keep going beyond the three weeks, but I knew I had to give it enough time to evaluate it, and I got back from Sedona the week of Thanksgiving and decided I'd give it until Christmas.

That's honestly the reason I landed on three weeks as a trial period. Sorry for those waiting for me to shed some magical facts about the science of habits. Thanksgiving to Christmas just felt right.

FIGURING OUT WHAT TO DO

I was extremely uncomfortable with starting something like this without some kind of framework. I went to my desk, located in my kitchen, clearly in pursuit of a pen and paper. I opened the top drawer and discovered half a dozen local magazines (SLO Life Magazine, for any SLOcals reading). What you don't know, and what's too damn ironic not to mention here, is that for the last decade, I've been a columnist for a local magazine covering outdoor adventures and fun experiences I recommend people try. Yet here I was at 34 without a damn clue of how to spend the luxurious two hours a day I was supposed to magically find for twenty-one consecutive days.

The idea seized me. What if I just redid some of these adventures I wrote about? I flipped through the pages and wrote down all the adventures that didn't require spending money, because I knew I was walking on thin ice as it was by paying for nannies to watch the kids while I didn't produce work.

Here is what I was left with:

- ~~Train Ride to Paso Robles~~
- Picnic at the Pismo Preserve
- Flotation therapy
- ~~Feeding Farm Animals at Avila Valley Barn~~
- ~~Ravine Waterpark in Paso Farm~~

Great, only two ideas. And that's how it started. Two ideas from articles I'd written months ago, thinking I was the local queen of fun experiences everyone should try.

FIRST SEVEN DAYS

If I was a journaler, I would have made these entries for Week 1:

Day 1:

Today I peed in a jar in my car, in front of what I can only hope was an empty office building. Not once, but three times. Turns out my bladder thinks starting meditating is a trigger for peeing.

I searched YouTube for anything about learning how to develop my intuition. Twenty-three minutes of searching, buffering, not liking, searching, buffering, accidentally clicking a creepy one, which sent me back to browsing through endless content all promising me magic pills and quick breakthroughs. Finally, I found someone who seems more happy-hippie-yoga than earthy-crystal-ball-mystic. It doesn't hurt that she had an Australian accent. I may even stay awake for the full 20 minutes.

What do you know? I did my first meditation for more than three minutes, and this one was awesome. I think they call it a guided meditation. I didn't have to sit there trying NOT to think. They actually told me to think and guided me on what to think. I feel like I just unleashed my imagination and had a party in my brain.

I found one more meditation, which was also awesome! I can't believe I'm liking this. Then I watched a quick educational video about what they call Clairs, or ways Spirit communicates to us.

HOLY SHIT, I think I do have them all, and this is blowing my mind. I can literally go back in time and remember how I received messages that I just disregarded and later regretted. This is wild. I'm obsessed with this.

I'm so pumped right now. I know I'm not in a sweet-ass She Shed or a cool office somewhere. I'm just in my CRV in a commercial parking lot. But it feels amazing to be alone, to be in peaceful silence. What a great way to start the day.

Day 2:

I checked off a hike on my list. :) It only has two things on it, but who cares. I hiked the Pismo Preserve! Forgot to bring water. Definitely christened some lucky plants on the way, but the view was so life-giving. I can't put into words how much it fed my soul to stand up and look at a panoramic view of the ocean sparkling in the sun. To feel the sunshine on my skin. It was magic.And during a Tuesday workday at 10 am What is my life? This is wild, but so freaking awesome.

Is this what life would have been like if I'd actually lived up to what my fellow 8th graders voted for me, "Most likely to be a gold digger?"

I sat up there soaking it in, listening to relaxing music. Soaking it all in, not in any rush. Nowhere to run to, just sitting there enjoying myself with no one yelling at me to help them.

I love having two whole hours because it's just enough time to actually drive 15 minutes to an epic 45-minute round-trip hike and then still have time to drive to the office without stress. Whoever came up with two hours is a genius. It's just enough time to do something fun and NOT be rushed. That's worth so much to me right now. I forgot what having time felt like.

Day 3:

It was rainy and cold (55 degrees and windy! Yuck), so I went back to the deserted parking lot, did some more meditations around intuition, and then tried some Wim Hof breath work that Angel Guide Rick had recommended.

Holy moly. I felt light, airy, and suddenly free of stress. Is this what drugs feels like? This is incredible. Only took me 11 minutes. I'm seriously in the best mood.

Day 4:

This feels hard. I just wanted to connect to Spirit and have a cool spiritual experience, maybe hear a voice of truth or that quiet voice I've heard a couple times would come through. I sit here in stillness, and it's not coming today. What am I doing wrong? Is something wrong with me? Why is this so hard? It felt like I was making some progress before, but today I just spent two hours trying to connect and getting frustrated it didn't happen right away.

Ugh, is this even working?

I ditched my car and all the meditations and decided to go on a hike. Still no voices, but I felt slightly less stuck.

It's been annoying me all day, and I've been thinking about why I struggled, and then I had to laugh at myself a little because here I am trying to focus on BEING not DOING, and all I feel today is frustration that I'm not accomplishing what I want.

Maybe I need to drop the goal of having on-demand connection to my intuition. Maybe I need to just play and enjoy the two hours and focus on that?

Day 5:

Okay, it's Friday. Sunny and I'm out on a hike I haven't done since I was a freshman in the dorms. It was insane how I passed certain parts of the trail and could recall the conversation I was having with a friend the last time I hiked here. Memory is wild.

Then I decided to listen to some low key music, and I found some cool, vibey music from some Spotify playlist called Divine Feminine.

Lots of chanting, which I wasn't super into, but I discovered a group called Beautiful Chorus and couldn't help myself. I stood on the side of Felsman's Loop and started to dance, interpretive style. It felt amazing to move to music in the sunlight. I forgot how much joy dance brings me. I must have been dancing for half an hour because I cut my hike a little short and still made it back to the car to do some of that Wim Hof breathwork, and I feel superhuman. No joke. This is insane energy.

I'm having so much fun. I don't know what could phase me. Also, think I may need to find my sunscreen because I'm already getting sunburned on my forehead in December. How is this real life?

Day 6:

It's 10 pm and just finished my two hours. Whew! I did it, and it was awesome, but what a shit show today was. It was the first weekend I tried to take two hours and it was so much harder than the work week. Work is easier for me to step away from than family. I kept waiting for the "right time" to present itself, and it never came. Michael had to work in the morning and then we had fun Christmas things I'd planned weeks ago. I just struggled to ask for the time and felt resentful everyone seemed to forget I had this new commitment to myself. Then I was angry at myself for not having negotiated for my sacred time, but also I felt so guilty leaving my kids on the weekend. They were used to me being gone during the week, but the weekend was my time with them.

But I finally made it happen in the 11th hour. I didn't have a space to retreat to to spend time alone. I didn't have a plan for evening alone time. Michael watched Netflix in the living room, and so it was either bedroom or kitchen for me.

So I went to the kitchen and decided that since I had so much fun dancing on my hike yesterday that maybe I could light some candles and just listen to that Divine Feminine playlist and dance in the kitchen.

Two hours. Dancing in my kitchen. It was amazing. The time flew by, and I just had so much childish joy. I can't believe I haven't danced more as an adult. I feel like a kid again.

Going to bed tired, but happy.

Day 7:

I planned better today, thankfully. Sent the family to run errands, which Michael was stoked about because he'd been wanting to go to Home Depot and Costco, and the kids love those stores (masks and all). I just hiked the hill behind our house, climbed a tree, and sat in silence listening to birds chirp. The mockingbird is for sure my favorite to listen to. Birds are so cheerful. I could watch them for hours.

Then I decided to explore the hillside. I hugged trees, touched plants, smiled and twirled in the morning sunlight, watch clouds, and then I wanted to listen to a meditation and found something interesting on YouTube. It's called a walking meditation. It was so powerful. Perfectly blended what I've liked so far—nature, check. Sunshine, check. Meditation, check. Movement, check.

I'm even back before the family, and I have the house all to myself and feel so excited to see them and enjoy my family day. This has been such an amazing week. Glad I have two more.

EVERYTHING I TRIED IN THREE WEEKS

I can safely say that the following two weeks further expanded the list of things I was finding joy in.

Three Week Self-Care List:

- Guided meditations for developing my intuition
- Visualizing my dream life meditations
- I AM Affirmations audio

- Learn about auras and chakras
- Hike to beautiful peaks nearby
- Enjoy nature
- Climb a tree
- Dance in nature
- Dance in the kitchen in candlelight
- Listen to walking meditation
- Read a book in the sunshine
- Breath work
- Sit by the ocean and enjoy listening to the waves

I tracked what activities brought me the most joy and which ones didn't feel restorative. I found that while I love to learn, I could listen to podcasts while I made breakfast or get ready, (when the kids watch cartoons) and then I'd have some things to process and think through when I got on my two hours.

I learned to plan ahead, to negotiate ahead of the day for the best window of time on the weekend. I learned to be flexible if the ideal window wasn't likely.

I showed up on the days I didn't know what to do. I showed up in the evenings on days I just couldn't make it happen. I kept going when I had severe mom guilt, promising myself that I'd be happier as a mom once I went. Which, so far, was definitely true.

And, of course, I got bored and had to change things up. I didn't want to become too routine with my two hours. I wanted it to stay fresh and exciting because I wanted to keep the momentum going, and getting bored is the surest way for me to quit something.

MY THREE WEEK TRANSFORMATION

But the important part was I had committed to a 21-day sprint of self-care, and I didn't give up on myself. I would tear up thinking about that. I didn't flake on me.

Just that alone time sent pride up through my spine daily. I was so damn proud of myself. I was grinning like someone who had completed a marathon. Because when you have conditioned yourself for decades to betray your needs … the day you throw a stake in the ground and say "I deserve to be prioritized" is the day you feel like you won a gold medal.

Taking two hours is like hitting a giant PAUSE button on our hectic lives. It's been so profound that after just doing it for three weeks, I saw my life transform. Michael did too, and so did my kids. I felt like a completely different person. (So cliche, but it's exactly how it felt.)

My highlight reel of what benefits happened for me within three weeks of spending two hours a day in solitude:

- I was happy every single day.
- I was initiating having sex, daily.
- I didn't care if it was a weekend or weekday, as long as I took two hours.
- I felt free again.
- I felt playful and childlike.
- Low grade anxiety was gone.
- Depression was gone.
- I lost stubborn weight.
- I had incredible energy every day.
- I saw opportunity and beauty everywhere.
- I felt optimistic, like anything could happen.
- I felt so grateful.
- I was so proud of myself for sticking with it.
- I felt sexy.

- I felt creative.
- I felt unstoppable.
- I stopped feeling like a victim and embraced that I'm the creator of my destiny.
- I felt confident.

I WASN'T GOING TO STOP

Then it hit me. I wasn't stopping. I think I knew it on Day 8. I was finally acquainted with being prioritized and cared for, and I wasn't going to let myself off the hook. I had changed so much. I couldn't stomach the idea of going back to the control freak, burnout queen who was so unhappy. I would never trade on my happiness ever again. It was off the table.

What is crazy to think back on was how three weeks earlier, I'd asked permission to take care of myself. Seriously? I'd collapsed on the damned kitchen floor and almost crashed my car from fatigue midday, and I was still negotiating for what I needed.

In our sick culture we negotiate for things like health, well-being, and sanity. These are considered luxuries. Meanwhile, I knew for sure if I suddenly had to work two extra hours a day to hit a deadline or bring in a new client, NO ONE would question it. In fact, I'd be praised for my hustle.

We can't negotiate for our health and happiness, but wealth-building and hustle,hat's allowed? How ass-backwards is that?

And I started this whole journey negotiating.

We only ask for permission as authorities in our own lives when we're anticipating being judged or punished. And I knew the silent rules around "getting extra time". It had to be productive, it had to be revenue generating, or it was labeled "nice to have" not "have to have," and "nice to haves" only can last so long.

Our self-worth is so deeply tied to earning money and working hard, especially in this country.

In three weeks I shifted from a woman who needed permission to a full-blown, self-care vigilante who knew my health and wellness would never be placed on the negotiation table again. I felt like Patrick Swayze's voice was in my head saying, "Nobody puts Paden's wellbeing in the corner." Nope, it was center stage now, and damn that felt good.

Needless to say, with the results I experienced in three weeks, I didn't even ask for permission to continue. I just kept going. I had proven to myself that I could get more done in less time. I had proven my mental and physical health was improving and that I could be happier and enjoy my life if I spent focused time each day taking care of my soul. This wasn't a fad. It wasn't a challenge. It wasn't a milestone. Taking two was a lifestyle. It was critical to my growth journey and embracing the woman I was always designed to be, and it wasn't going anywhere. I didn't care what resistance was coming, and oh, I could feel it coming.

chapter 7
RISE OF THE RESISTANCE

"Every time you're given a choice between disappointing someone else and disappointing yourself, your duty is to disappoint that someone else. Your job, throughout your entire life, is to disappoint as many people as it takes to avoid disappointing yourself."
- Glennon Doyle, *Untamed*

The first time someone described San Luis Obispo to me, they said. "It's a cool college town just ten minutes from the beach. It's an outdoor lover's paradise." So I applied to the local university Cal Poly, got accepted, and the first time I walked on campus was the day I moved into the dorms. One of the things I always wanted to learn, as soon as I moved here, was how to surf. It was so iconic, and I felt like to be Californian, you should know how to surf, so in college when my friend Ben said he had an extra wet suit and a foam board and asked if I'd like to learn, I jumped at the chance.

Like anyone new at something, we started where I could be successful. Which was as far away from the water as possible. We started

on the sand. I practiced how to jump up on my board from the sand. That was awkward. Then we worked up to trying it in the whitewash. That was not easy either. But once I felt confident enough and could figure out how to jump up on my board and ride a 1 foot wave that instantly turned into whitewash, I felt like I may be able to surf.

That's when we ventured into the bigger waves. Of course, we picked sunny days with smaller surf to start, and I spent an entire two hours flailing around in waves like a dog who's just happy to be in water. The hard part for me about surfing is each wave is different, so it felt like the environment was ever-changing. At some point I just embraced that was part of it.I returned again and again to the ocean, determined to surf. It took me all summer.

When I think about my brief stint in life as a "surfer girl," there is one memory that comes up for me—the time I got caught in a huge set and couldn't get out. I want you to picture 8 feet; it's the size of a typical Christmas tree or step ladder, not super huge as waves go, until you imagine your head being where the rug is, then looking up at an 8 foot wave barreling towards you and it starts to feel like a huge wall of water. (Honestly it's terrifying and exhilarating all at the same time.)

I'll never forget how crazy I felt watching the waves that day. I was watching the timing of the waves, trying to find the break in the set and how long I'd have before it started again. You see, to even ride a wave you have to paddle out past the break, and waves come in sets. Typically a wave set could be three to ten large waves, aand there is typically a resting period between them, which can last between 5 and 25 minutes, so I was waiting to see when I could go.

I waited, and when I counted the start of the next set, I started to paddle out. I paddled for what felt like an hour and barely progressed 10 yards. I put all my attention into paddling and stopped watching the waves. My timing sucked. I had barely made it out to where the set was already breaking. I could either wait to be pushed back again and have to redo the intense paddle I'd already done, or I could push through and duck dive underneath some of the waves, hoping this was the end of the set. I chose to keep going. And when I ducked with my board under the wave, by the time I came up for air, a huge wave crashed right onto me, sending me far below into the ocean. I went limp, like they say, and let the current carry me up. I gasped for air and caught the next wave in the face. Back down again I went. This went on for at least six waves, and my lungs were screaming for air. And then the set ended. I caught my breath, paddled out, and mustered up the courage to try to surf an 8-foot wave. I saw the first slow-rolling wave coming, and I started to paddle out to the beach. I timed it perfectly. And thankfully for me it wasn't nearly the size of the previous waves. It was probably closer to 5 feet, and I dropped right in and rode that wave! I was so exhausted and so thrilled with myself. I rode it all the way until it became white wash, and I collapsed on the beach in happiness.

I learned that the joys of surfing outweighed the discomfort of paddling out.

When I think about what I faced with trying to take two hours a day, for me it felt like getting caught in those waves and having to push my way through to be able to experience the joy of carving out time each day to feel happy and free.

This has not been easy. At times my feeling of resistance was constant, but I fought like hell and kept going. I'd be doing you a great disservice if I acted like all it took was me giving myself permission to change my life. It's certainly part of it, but it also took facing down my fears of rejection, my compulsion to people please, and testing how much I really believed I was worth it.

Over the course of this journey, I was met with resistance that came in sets, resistance from many different places. Sometimes it felt like it was all at once, and sometimes I caught my breath. Eventually I got stronger, stronger because of the waves of resistance that showed up.

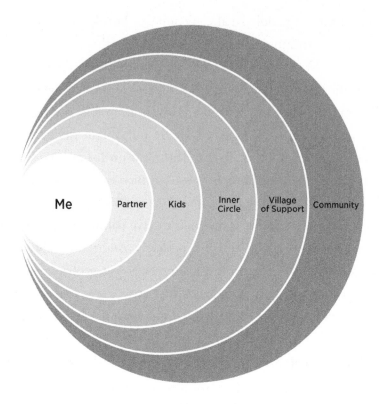

- First wave in the set of resistance was me.
- Second wave in the set was my partner Michael.
- Third wave was my kids.
- Fourth wave was my inner circle (chosen, birth, and inherited family).
- Fifth wave was my village of support (employees, nannies, and clients).
- Last wave was my community.

As much as each group wanted to support me, cheered for me at times and offered support, each also presented resistance to my resolve to continue taking two hours a day beyond my three-week trial.

RESISTANCE WAVE 1: ME

Resistance for me always shows up in negative self-talk through the voices of Bitchy Brittany and Pleasing Prudence. Both voices pop up in every day moments to "put me back" into my conditioned state, the one that's smaller, conforming, and in too much survival mode to be truly activating for others.

I'd wake up on a weekend and this thought would pop up, "Is it selfish of me to ask for this time?"

I'd watch unread emails mount up and a thought would pop up, "Do I deserve this kind of time alone? Imagine how much you'd get done if you worked through the two hours?"

My kids would ask me why I work so much, and I'd think, "Am I neglecting my family? Being a bad mom or a selfish wife?"

I'd sit out in nature and feel a little antsy in the beginning because of this unhappy thought, "How long will I be able to put up with not being productive?"

And when I thought about my health issues and how slowing down seemed to be the common advice, I'd secretly think, "Isn't there a pill you could take?" That would have been easier.

I'd look back through my phone late at night and love seeing Kennedy as a baby or remember how little the kids had been and reflect on how big they were growing, and I'd think, "Taking two hours a day is fourteen more hours a week I'm not spending with my kids. They are only young once. Will I live to regret this?"

I'd walk into work at 11 am and instantly think, "Does the team think I'm a prima donna?" Needless to say, it happened a lo, in varied frequency. Now it's not as much, but in the beginning it was daily.

If we haven't already established that, I have been a chronic people pleaser for most of my life. It showed up big time in my resistance to self-care. It boiled down to caring what others thought about me and not wanting to be an inconvenience to anyone.

Here's the thing, when you set any goal like this in your life that requires time, everyone with demands on your time will be disappointed at some point. It's the side effect to anticipate when people pleasers like me finally learn that, "No is a full sentence." (Thanks Mel Robbins for that timely reminder.)

But I finally made peace that I'd rather disappoint others than disappoint myself, and I'd tell myself that damned near every day.

RESISTANCE WAVE 2: INTIMATE PARTNER

If there is anyone who has skin in the game when it comes to your personal growth and getting a handle on your mental health, it's your life partner. Michael had so much more to gain if taking two hours helped me. Thankfully he saw a glimpse of that from day one and was more supportive than most. I truly can't thank him enough. When it came down to who this lifestyle change would impact the most, that was him too. He took on a greater parenting role on weekends. He worried about what my working 10 hours less per week would mean to our business, that still needed to survive a pandemic, our business that was his life's dream. He still had to look over the family finances and see how much we pay nannies and know that 40 hours a month of paying for nannies was simply so I could be outside dancing in nature in the name of happiness, and he watched my life and happiness improve, doing something for myself that he hadn't yet given himself permission to do.

Knowing all this, I was sensitive to any comment about my taking two hours a day. Comments like:

"Do you feel like it's fair to take your two hours during the weekend? Am I supposed to pick up the slack on the weekends?" "You'd really rather go dance in the kitchen than snuggle on the couch with me?"

Or side comments like, "You barely work anymore" and "Do you even get emails anymore?"

A handful of times this boiled up into a hard-headed clash of values. The biggest one and the one I least expected was around vacation. About six months into my lifestyle of taking two hours for myself, we decided to take a family vacation to Mexico. It was a seven-day vacation.

One night on our weekly date night we were talking about what we're looking forward to the most, and among other things, I mentioned how excited I was to take my two hours on the beach in the morning. "What? You're actually planning to take two hours on our family vacation?"

"Yes. Why wouldn't I? It's my recipe for happiness, and I want to be happy on vacation."

"I thought being with your family on vacation would make you happy."

"It's awesome, but with little kids it's more like a trip than a vacation. I still get overwhelmed and irritated without alone time. Every vacation with the kids feels exhausting. I really need this time."

Cue the awkward pause. The change of subject and the uncomfortable drive home followed. He was not happy. While I express when I'm unhappy, he shoves it down, but it was felt.

When we got home, I tried to understand his perspective, while telling myself my well-being was not coming off the table.

What I had failed to understand was that we had different definitions of vacation. I was viewing vacation like a string of seven weekend days, meaning I'd get my two hours like usual. Michael was viewing it as the only time we get to connect as a family all year, meaning there was no need for me to escape for two hours, but I still wanted my time, and he wanted time together, and both are good motives. I also sensed that there was something deeper going on.

Finally Michael said, "I just need to know that you'll sacrifice for me if I need you to, like I've sacrificed for you. Are you willing to compromise for me?"

There it was, and I absorbed his need to feel seen and have a partner who wasn't only advocating for herself. It didn't mean I couldn't advocate for myself, but he needed me to support his needs, and as someone who for years shut my mouth when I knew I needed something, I had to honor what he was doing. I was certainly happy to support his need for family time, as long as it didn't cost me what I needed.

So I said, "What if I took my two hours when you're all still asleep? Like I leave at 5 am and come back at 7 am for breakfast?"

"The kids wake up at 6 am."

"Yes they do, and all they want to do is watch cartoons for a little while. That gives you time to get your espresso and go outside and enjoy time to read, then I'd be back when breakfast arrives."

"That could work."

"And what if you took two hours as well? What if we switched off?"

He tried on that idea, and smiled, "That actually sounds nice."

So there it was, our new way of vacationing.

Now as long as we're telling the truth, the first morning on vacation where my alarm woke me up at 4:45 am, I was annoyed as hell. Maybe it was that I had to grab clothes in the dark room, smacked my head on the bathroom linen closet door, and sleuthed my way out of the room like I was doing something wrong. Ugh! This was not feeling very magical, but what I'd forgotten was that on the Caribbean side of Mexico, the sun rises over the water, and it ended up being such a special memory because every morning I woke up and walked out to the beach in darkness and got to spend two hours watching the symphony of colors light up the sky, it was pure magic. Okay, I conceded ,5 am is worth it.

Michael loved taking two hours and every night would talk about what he'd like to do with his time the next day, and watching and supporting him through that process without self-betraying my needs for my own time was incredibly liberating.

The cherry on the cake came a year after I'd been taking two hours, when I stepped down as CEO of our company (a different story for another time) and he stepped in as CEO. One of the first things he did was have our team block off his calendar for two hours a day. He calls it his CEO time.

RESISTANCE WAVE 3: CHILDREN

Leaving my kids was something I knew how to do as a working mom, but before taking two hours, I was leaving them to go to work to afford the lifestyle we had and wanted to give them. I had worked a long time to reduce my mom guilt around working. Leaving them to go and take care of myself was a new thing, and new things require new thought patterns and new inner pep talks to justify.

One day it had been really hard to leave the kids. I finally snuck out and started to think about what I wanted to do that day for my two hours. I walked down the block, and then I heard a familiar voice call out, "MAMA!!!!" I turned and looked and saw my daughter running down the street crying, bare feet on cold pavement, in a nightgown, chasing me down. I wrapped her up in a big hug and promised I'd come back. I kissed her hand and told her to hold it over her heart when she missed me to feel how much I loved her. She took a deep breath and kissed me before I walked her back to the front door, where her brother and nanny waited. She waved bravely, and I assured her I loved her and would be back at 2:30.

Once out of sight, I teared up on the way to my car. I got into the car, and my mind was tortured with Pleasing Prudence and Bitchy Brittany.

You're the mom. You're different. She needs you more than she needs her dad.

You're so selfish. How could you leave after that? You are taking this two-hour thing too seriously. It's impacting your kids.

I sobbed all the way to the trailhead to hike up to my favorite view, and that's when the fire of my righteous anger showed up as my protector.

I deserve to have time to myself.

I am safeguarding my mental health so I can be a better mom for her.

I am modeling how it is to take care of myself. She's highly sensitive too, and I'm showing her how to respect our need for alone time. A happy mom is better than an ever-present mom. This makes me happy. Do I want her to remember me as the mom who was always there, always irritable with unpredictable mood swings, or the mom who was happy whenever she showed up? Keep going. It's going to get easier.

And I found my way out of the car, feeling sad and angry. Ninety minutes later I walked down from the mountain inspired, happy, and rejuvenated, and that feeling right there kept me going.

My kids continued to resist my two-hour habit. My verbal child, Kennedy, who was between three and five years old when this was going on was the most resistant.

"Why can't I come Mommy?"

"Because I need to be alone."

"Why do you need to be away from me?"

"It's not that I need to be away from you. I just need to be away with me."

"Okay, how about if I come and quietly read books?"

"No, Honey, Mommy needs time to be alone and to take care of myself, and when you're with me, I like to be able to focus on taking care of you. Everyone needs to be taken care of and needs to learn how to take care of themselves. I am learning how to do that now."

"Okay, Mommy, but I'll miss you." Disappointment in her tone.

Those conversations were tough, but then I found a way to make it empowering and started to tell her how important it is for each of us to learn to enjoy time alone and know how to make ourselves happy without relying on anyone else to do that for us. I'd ask her how she likes to take care of herself. Before too long, I'd come home and ask where Kennedy was, and her nannies would say, "She said she needed alone time and has been in her room happily reading to herself."

My heart soared, and of course, I teared up the first time I heard that. This habit mattered. It was far bigger than me. It was role modeling for my kids to advocate for themselves and learn to rely on themselves for their happiness, not other people.

And now if I'm a little sharp in my tone or my energy is off, Kennedy is the first to look at me and ask, "Mom, did you get your alone time today?"

She knows. She knows it works, and she knows her mom is a happier mom because of it.

RESISTANCE WAVE 4: INNER CIRCLE

I speak about this later in *Take Two*, but the true voices that rose up in resistance were not the men in my life; it was the women in my life. Classic, right?

One hidden blessing of all this was that this transformation took place during the pandemic, where contact was more limited and very few held a true front-row seat to the unfolding of this journey outside of my immediate family, but when the world started to ease back into social events, that's when most of the resistance came with it.

Here's what I've concluded. When you seek to redefine your self-worth, just that act alone triggers the people closest to you because it puts a mirror up for them, making them think about how they show up for themselves or don't, and that can feel angering and invasive to those who haven't decided they want or need to change their life. The thing is, they don't mean to provide resistance, and you aren't intentionally trying to hold up a mirror. It's just what happens.

So I'd go to a wedding and someone from my inner circle would ask what's new and I'd share the update on my journey, to which they'd quickly respond in a dismissive tone, "I don't personally need that alone time. That's so nice you've found something that helps you."

I'd be in a Zoom call with my bad-ass female entrepreneur besties, and someone would admit, "Yeah, when I first heard you were taking two hours every day I was so triggered. Seriously."

Or I'd be at dinner with a couple, and the wife would turn to me and say, "Do you let Michael take two hours a day for himself? or Do you only get that alone time?"

To which I'd respond, "He doesn't need my permission. If he decides that's what he needs, I'm happy to support him."

I'd go on a podcast and be vulnerable in my message and get a text from someone close to me that read, "It was good to hear in that podcast Michael's actual response to you taking that kind of time off each day. Of course he'd struggle with it."

And most of the time it was just a topic that soon became a topic to avoid. The silence and lack of response around my sharing what I was doing for myself was not missed. Mind you, this was not everyone close to me. Obviously many of my inner circle have been proud of me and encouraging, but I'm highlighting the resistance because I want you to know this wasn't easy for me. It's not easy to be excited about a journey you're on, one that is changing your life, and have people side step discussing it in conversation, or I became the person they even awkwardly avoid or just straight up give you the cold shoulder at events because "you've changed too much."

Yep, when you step into self-improvement habits of any kind and gain any traction, it'll challenge those around you. Change enough, and it'll threaten everyone who benefited from the person you were before, and trust me, it's always fascinating to discover who liked you better when you were unhappy inside.

RESISTANCE WAVE 5: MY VILLAGE AND TEAM

I believe it takes a village of support for me to be able to run successful businesses, raise happy kids, and still put meaningful work into the world. I don't believe I'm alone in that. Nope, it takes a system of support to allow dreamers to put dreams into the world.

For me our team of supporters comprise our nannies and employees. Every nanny who has loved my kids, taken them to parks while I worked and said yes to staying longer so I could finish a chapter of this book, are beyond valued in my world. Every team member who picked up the tasks I clearly had to delegate as soon as I decided to cut down my workday to four hours was absolutely essential to this journey.

But everyone has a life outside of my dreams, and team members still have goals to hit. For me, the primary resistance from our employees and team members came in the form of struggling with my work-life balance. For me to pull this off, I had to get aggressive with my personal and work boundaries, and I did.

This made it harder than usual for me. If a nanny called in sick or would ask me if they could come later that day, I had to run a tight ship to get everything done and not miss meetings, client appointments, and fit in my two hours. Before all this, I'd just work late at night, but

I'd find myself often faced with picking between two hours or work obligations because I was home with the kids all day.

The same thing made it harder for our team members and employees. I was less accessible. I was in the office less, and during all this, I made a career change to get back to consulting and professional coaching, so then I had to add more responsibilities to my plate while still helping Michael run our fitness business.

Resistance didn't come in attitudes. It doesn't come in snide comments. It came in the form of emails and texts. My team would ask, "Can I schedule that important meeting next Thursday? I see you have a time block called 'I deserve two hours.' Can I book it then?"

My clients would email, "Can we move our consulting meeting? I have—insert super important high-level event? Do you have tomorrow at—insert time slot I have dedicated for my two hours?"

My team would text me and say, "I know you said you wanted to have a meeting with X employee that was really important. I can't find time for the two of you to meet until six weeks from now, unless you move your two hours."

Then I'd hear through the grapevine that part of what was happening when goals weren't hit was that I was "hard to get a hold of" or team members were waiting for a reply and didn't know when I was coming in.

And I'd breathe deeply and tell myself that I had to learn how to have and hold boundaries. It was vital to my well-being. So I held it 90% of the time, which was a vast improvement, but it was so tempting each time I got a text, email to betray my personal values in the name of profit, progress, or urgency. Every time I held my boundary, it hit me deep in my high performer's heart. It tested my values, and probably the only reason I am writing this book is because my value of making my well-being a priority overtime became more important than making money, hitting goals, and achieving more accolades.

RESISTANCE WAVE 6: MY COMMUNITY

I live in a small town that we joke has two degrees of separation, meaning any stranger quickly turns into the friend of someone you've known for years after a short conversation. I'll never forget halfway through this journey when I was playing with my kids at a local park. It was 3 pm on Wednesday, and I had two hours with nowhere else to be, nothing else to do but just enjoy them. I was sliding down the slide with both kids on my lap, and we were laughing together and chasing each other around the park.

I couldn't help but notice how few of the mothers were playing with their kids. Instead, they were using the diversion of the park to catch up with themselves and get some treasured adult time, which left me and the nannies as the only adults on the play structures, but I was thirsty, so I headed to the drinking fountain and then recognized one of the women in the mom group. I hadn't seen her in years and went over to say hi. As we talked, she said, "I love following you on social media and seeing your posts about taking time for yourself. Is that what you're doing now?"

"Oh, no. I'm just done with my work day and playing with my kids."

"Oh, so this doesn't count as play time?" She looked confused.

"No, this is a fun playdate with the kids time." I smiled.

"Oh. I'm confused. When do you take your two hours? How do you fit it in if playing with your kids doesn't count?"

"I usually do it right when our nanny gets to our house and then I go to work after."

Another mom overheard and said, "Oh my gosh, are you that gym owner with a podcast that's taking two hours a day for self-care?" "Yes," my friend answered for me.

"That's just crazy! I don't even know what I'd do with two hours. I can barely find five minutes." All the moms threw their support behind this admission,.

I knew better than to take the opportunity to become an evangelist for my life-changing habit.

"It must be nice for you to have that. I wish I could do that," said the third mom in the circle.

I still honestly don't have a great response to comments that make it seem like doing this was easy or that it's a privilege few can experience, because while I recognize my privilege, I firmly believe every one of us in a burned out, reactionary state easily wastes two hours a day just zoning out or not focusing. Which means we have opportunities to shift using that time for self-care. But throughout my journey on social media or in my larger community, I got used to resistance like,

"Word on the street, amongst the moms in SLO, is that you're taking two hours a day for self-care. So do you work anymore?"

"Must be nice for you to take this time each day. I wish I could."

"I don't think my husband would let me take that much time for myself. How did you word it so he'd let you?"

"You know your whole two-hour thing, it honestly sounds horrible to me. I hate spending time alone."

And then the conversation that makes me really uncomfortable, "So is working out part of your two hours?"

I'd admit that I didn't use that time to work out. I used it to slow down and relax.

And they'd look confused, "So you don't workout ever? When do you workout?"

"I don't. I hike. I walk. I dance. But I don't attend a workout class." It always made me so self-conscious because I was juggling all I could and was still getting messages that "it wasn't enough" because I'd cut out workouts, and I'd done it as someone who owns a fitness facility.

The waves of resistance came in sets and had a cadence that continues to this day. Although now it's in the form of asking if I'm still doing two hours a day, and I watch surprise wash over everyone's face when I say it's part of my lifestyle.

That's what it is. It's not a short-term thing. I treat it like a prescription to my health and happiness.

And who I'd become through the process of testing this idea to creating room for it permanently in my life was incredible. I went from asking for permission to put my health needs first to setting a three-week test and showing up every day to a self-care advocate who paddled in the face of opposition and kept going because I finally believed I deserved happiness and well-being in this life.

THE JOURNEY CONTINUES

My three-week test had been so game-changing, I kept going. As I progressed through the year, there became an ebb and flow to taking two hours.

The first couple of months I was obsessed with meditating and wanted so badly to discern how my intuition best worked and how to make it reliable for me. I learned a lot about how my intuition worked. For the first time, I realized that I am not my body or my thoughts. I am my soul. Meditation gave me the ability to know that to be true and to be able to separate my thoughts from my spirit's quiet voice. That's when I realized how spirit has always spoken to me, through thoughts, sensations, and visualizations.

The next couple months I realized how happy I was in nature, and I went on every hike in our town I could think of. Many of those trails I hadn't hiked since I was a freshman at Cal Poly. It's amazing how I could pass a boulder and recall all the sunset nights I spent climbing it with my college boyfriend, probably overanalyzing how to figure him out.

But here I was at thirty-four years old, finally realizing the power of just letting my mind wander.

The next couple months I really started to want to feed my mind with new philosophical and spiritual messages to spend time considering, so I'd drive to beautiful lookouts over the Pacific ocean and use the 15-minute car drive to listen to something. Then I'd go out into nature and think on my own about what I'd listened to and consider it's meaning. I also had a solid decade of personal development content I'd consumed and not really thought too much about. I was always in a state of waterboarding myself with new information. So this season, I went back to the archives of my brain and really sorted through a lot of concepts, and many of them finally had time to take root in my heart and make the desired impact. I was in a full state of processing during these months.

Toward the one-year mark, it all simplified. I found my go-to three or four things I love to do that bring me the most joy and energy, and I do those. I meditate, have a manifesting dance I do to specific music, wander in beautiful landscapes, and tune into my intuition, and connect to God directly in my own way.

The thing I can promise you is that while you think you're just meditating or hiking more, when you give yourself this kind of time to wonder and process your thoughts, the topics that rise to the surface are so profound. I truly believe that we are all self-healers. If you can get alone and start to face some of the harder things in life, you can, over time, make profound changes.

This is exactly what Part Two of this book is dedicated to. In each chapter, I share one of the top profound transformations I experienced as a result of disciplining myself to spend two solitary hours alone each day for an entire year and a half. Each chapter tackles a huge area in my life that I would have said before was "just fine." And in denying the pain and dysfunction that was there for decades, huge areas in my life sat unimproved for far too long.

Getting time each day to step away from the noise and to tune into my own inner wisdom, lead me to explore radical shifts in my life. It shifted me from feeling stuck to being on a mission.

I can't wait to share what I learned in the next section, because when I say my life transformed, the juiciest and more profound ways my two-hour habit changed, we haven't even talked about yet.

PART 2

The Undoing

"The undoing is almost always more difficult than the doing."
- Kate DiCamillo

There is a part of us that is pure, untouched and a glorious embodiment of wisdom and innocence. That's the part we came into this world so closely aligned with, and I'm convinced the journey to healing as an adult is making our way back to that place. To do that requires a great undoing. Undoing of the conditioning, undoing of the generational programming and social constructs that lead us to feeling so disconnected from our hearts and souls that we don't even know how to express how we feel or why we are so numb.

The thing about Undoing is you rarely know exactly what needs to be undone. You just take time to witness yourself, name your true feelings, and allow curiosity to lead you down the paths you need to undo to come back home to yourself. That's exactly what I did.

chapter 8
THE MOTHERLOAD

**"If airplane safety videos have taught me anything,
David, it's that a Mother puts her own mask on first."
- Moira Rose, *Schitt's Creek***

ONE MONTH TAKING TWO:
That Damned Elsa Crown

At the beginning of this book I shared about my daughter's heartbreakingly cute habit of sending me off to work with "something to remember her by." A token of her love.

Well, Month 1 into what was now going beyond a simple three-week experiment and becoming my daily two-hour sanity check, I found myself staring at the Elsa crown she had handed me so I "wouldn't forget her."

In all fairness, she'd been doing this since Jackson was born, over a year of being reminded that my daughter is afraid I'll forget her because I leave for work. I didn't like it, but I'd gotten used to it. But ever since taking two hours for myself, it hit differently.

Before I'd tell her, "I have to go to work," like I was a victim, but now the truth was staring me in the face. I was choosing to leave, and not just for work, to be alone and prioritize myself. And as much as I tried to pep talk myself into believing I was some role model of female empowerment by finally doing something for my well-being … some days I just felt pregnant with self-judgement and doubt. Some days I felt like I may as well have had my forehead stamped "selfish."

I sat there in my driveway, eating slowly into my sacred two hours. But I felt torn on whether to disregard this feeling coming up in me, and just do what I always did with uncomfortable feelings—push it down and hope it stayed there.

Then I heard the cheerful sounds of the kids and their nanny playing in the front yard, and I freaked out like a teenager late for curfew.

What if I get caught?

Caught by who? I'm a grown ass woman.

I was fully annoyed with myself, and I quickly backed up the driveway and drove to the nearest hike to "hike it out."

An hour and a half and 3 miles later, I was back in a good mood and no longer feeling guilty. Thank you sunshine and endorphins, my true cheerleaders on this journey to health.

THREE MONTHS TAKING TWO:
Processing Mom Rage, Hikers Beware

Starting a hike pissed off at life is a sure fire way to work through some shit. There's something about movement and thinking that are linked. If you can do something mindless like walking long distances, with space and time to process your feelings, it's better than therapy. (Sorry to the therapists reading this!)

But there I was, pissed about how fucked up modern motherhood can be.

Going from entrepreneur to entrepreneur mom had been a difficult transition for me. I was already burdened with insane expectations for myself as a professional and as a person trying to get to the root of my burnout, anxiety, and depression, and break generational patterns I didn't want to pass along, but adding kids tipped the scale for me.

What no one tells you is that when you become a mom there is NO break, and all those windows of discretionary time I'd taken for granted pre-kids had vanished. After eight weeks at home, I was losing myself *and* my mental health. I wasn't happier. I was drowning, and I couldn't show up as the mom I wanted to be, which led me to an unpopular opinion: I believe a happy mom is better than a constantly around mom. (There, I said it.)

This path couldn't be either a private or personal decision. Oh no. It was met with public commentary. As a working mom, I was constantly being asked where my kids were. As if I'd absentmindedly left them out in the car. I mean, what did they think I'd respond with, "Oops! Thanks for asking me. It totally slipped my mind that my child is still in the car." I was trying to get a 10-hour work day done in five hours. I was one hundred percent focused and "on" with no breaks, often no food ,and pissed at myself for having Mommy Brain and forgetting basic pieces of information. I'd leave work feeling discouraged that I didn't get enough time and then walk right back into my house with a whole different kind of workload and list of to-dos.

No break, barely any sleep, eating if I could. Before this journey, showering alone qualified as self-care. I'd fallen off the bandwagon of friendship. Being both an entrepreneur and a mom left me daily feeling like I was being waterboarded with responsibilities and expectations, and I was always aware that this was my own choice, as well as the cost of my decision to try to "have it all".

I bottled up the pressure I placed on myself to be good enough as best as I could, but if anyone offered me platitudes like "this too will pass" or "you can't get these days back," I visualized throwing water on their face and storming out of the room to sob. I was incredibly sensitive to criticism and hiding deeply-rooted BIG feelings. Was it anger? No, it's more unflattering than that.

It was rage. Mom rage.

The first time I heard that phrase, my inner voice, who you've already met—Bitchy Brittany—came up loud and strong: *Maybe you shouldn't have had kids if you already had anger problems. Why didn't you handle your rage before you had kids and do us **all** a favor.*

Brittany totally missed the point.

Mom rage is the result of women trying to be good moms AND keep up with all the other social expectations, leaving us feeling like we are always failing everything at once. After growing up like collectors of impossible expectations, we get drop-kicked into motherhood one day and take those expectations and pile them on top of our heads, put on heels, and try to walk a runway next to our peers as society lines up waiting for us to make a spectacle of ourselves. We're supposedly in this together, yet feel completely alone. And all the while we try hard, pulling out of the stops like researching the organic snacks with the least amount of sugar. We constantly feel like we aren't good enough.

You can relate, right? But there is something worse going on under the surface. While externally we look overwhelmed, wound tight, maybe get judged as control freaks … deep down we're feeling one primary emotion: rage. And we sure as hell know what society does to "angry women," don't we? It's the most threatening thing to be labeled as a angry woman. We are programmed to repel angry women. In a world where violent sex offenders walk freely, women who retaliate against their rapists are sentenced and called dangerous. In a world where an angry male politician is seen as strong, an angry female politician is publicly shamed in meme-form and doesn't poll well. Anger is admired in men, seen as masculine and the type of strength required to take action, but in a woman, it's harsh, scary, unflattering and condemned publicly. For a woman, being "enraged" was equivalent to being marked with the letter "A". No one knows what to do with an angry woman, and so few bother to dig down into why she's so damn angry. No, that's the work we get to champion, especially given how prolific our collective anger is.

But we *are* angry.

We are angry that we've believed these lies too long, the lies that we torment ourselves with daily:

- Your needs come last. Trying to put yourself first means you're selfish.
- A mother is the embodiment of sacrifice, and she should embrace it and love every minute of it.
- When you serve others first, your "cup" will defy science and magically overflow with something other than despair and resentment.
- As soon as you become pregnant, your body belongs to the family.
- Your partner will pick up half of the household workload as soon as a baby enters the picture.

We sat in the audience for years, looking at the promise of stepping into the glory of motherhood. Once we got behind the veil we found a sisterhood of depletion and toxic positivity, the kind that doesn't need care when sick or need a break, where complainers are branded "bad moms."

Because the only phrase allowed to accompany sheer desperation is "it's worth it for the kids." But is it? Is it worth us running off of 1% of our capacity … for years? And the whole time we run on fumes, we also question our sanity, holding so many details and schedules in our brain that we start to question our intelligence and utility. We ultimately find ourselves melting down in tears at random moments during the day with no one to talk to about it.

There is no room in our language for a mother's pain.

Even the clinically validated term postpartum depression continues to be marginalized into old school slang of "baby blues," which just makes it so much worse.

There is no provision given for we domestic shrews who face the daily reality that we've failed, to think like a therapist, de-stress like a yogi, run a household like a CEO, budget like an accountant, intuitively read our family members minds (and moods and energies), are wet and ready at our partner's wink, and of course, being as needless as a doll.

Desperate for a lifeline of encouragement, we are thrown: "This too shall pass," and "It goes by so fast." But what everyone forgets who's past parenting little kids is it's not like a "summer that passes." Hell no. It's full on four years of college, with a victory lap PER child. So it's not passing any time soon once you've embarked on the journey. It's not as simple as "It'll pass." Maybe when you're eighty, it seems like a decade plus of your life passes fast, but when you're on year one, how does it sound to spend another nine years in pure stress and survival mode?

And the only things slipping away faster than our kids' years are our sanity and happiness.

The truth is: Moms are not okay.

Behind the anger is a deep sense of betrayal, a betrayal not by the patriarchy, (dare I say that?), not by the dads—betrayal by one another. Women have been letting ourselves down for decades. As friends. As mothers. As coworkers. Competing with one another. Silently struggling behind closed doors and only showing the highlight reel to each other. Generations of suppression and indoctrination have us shelving our needs and denying our pressures. It's left us suffering, believing we're alone and that we're the only ones who fail, every damned day. And in swallowing it and acceptance, we perpetrate it on our daughters' generation. Well, I'm not having it.

Whew! I'd made it back to the parking lot at the end of a passionate rant. I felt better; I had to admit that. Validated feelings have that effect. I didn't honestly know it was there. It only really flared when I was faced with a nasty comment or witnessed my friends getting so stressed out trying to be good enough moms that they were getting put on more medication so their bodies could keep up. But it was there, deep inside, and I had let it out and witnessed the pain.

And felt better for it.

FOUR TO FIVE MONTHS TAKING TWO:
The Process of Purging The Rage

I recognized two things over the two months following that initial rant. I was filled with mom rage. Even after getting some of it off my chest, there was more to explore and release, and I'd felt the release of rage hiking, so I focused my two hours on exploring it.

I took my rage with me into my two hours. I stared into the tide as it came in and climbed up trees to find new perches to rest on, and slowly, I started to confront my pain around motherhood. That quiet voice inside me would come out of hiding, finally able to get a word in. And miraculously, I'd listen. I'd think. I'd wonder about what I was missing in my own motherhood journey. I'd recognize my privilege in those moments. We have two well-paid bread winners in our house, with enough money to pay nannies to come to our home, and both children are healthy. So why was I feeling so much like a victim here?

I'd meditate on it; ruminate on it, often having no answers, just space to process and unpack, to clarify what feelings were mine and which ones I'd absorbed that didn't resonate. And I started to allow my inner observer to watch me and catch me in moments of rage. I started to build awareness on how rage showed up for me. The times I'd raise my voice at my kids for making a mistake that made us late ate going somewhere fun. But I'd ruin the mood because I was desperate to get them out of the house so I could have fun with them, dammit. And even after I apologized, I'd see how they looked up at me and feel shame rise in my throat. The times I'd get so fed up, I'd cave and give them candy or a third snack of the day just to stop the whining. And then they'd tell Michael when he would get home, and he'd look at me with raised eyebrows, clearly unimpressed, and I'd feel a surge of anger inside my chest, anger rising up to protect me from any perceived judgment.

How dare anyone critique me?

I'm a fucking survivor right now.

I'm doing my best. Can't anyone see that?

I'd complain to Michael so many times when he got home, like I'd really taken one for the team by staying at home more. I'd be ready to hand it off at 5 pm and then realize we still had to get through the two most stressful hours of the day: bedtime. Ahh! It was inescapable, and I felt trapped. Trapped and angry. Angry because I was supposed to be in maternal heaven, living my ultimate purpose, and it didn't feel like that at all.

And here I am putting those moments of deep shame and anger to words in a damned book. Hide me now.

I wanted to hide those feelings away. Those bad, unladylike feelings. But now instead of hiding them, I saved them, saved them for my two hours. That became my refuge for "bad" feelings.

But each time I retreated to my alone time, I gave my feelings the opportunity to run through me. Emotions are energy in motion, and they need to move through me or they'd get bottled up and show up later as dysfunction. So I let them move, and in doing, so I made space for new thoughts, new epiphanies, ones that felt like my own.

I'm not alone.

There are more moms that relate to what I've written than those who would rather smile a fake smile, like the Monterey moms in Big Little Lies.

There are more angry women now than ever before.

The pandemic sealed it.

We are sick of living with chronic fatigue and irritability.

We are over the brain fog that makes us the butt of belittling "mom brain" jokes.

We are done with embracing low grade anxiety as part of our personalities.

We are sick, literally sick in our bodies from prolonged stress.

We have enmeshed our identities so fully with those of our children that we've lost a sense of self.

But if we shut down, we are ostracized, pitied by other generations for making it so hard on ourselves, and slandered cruelly by other mom peers.

So what do we do? We stop taking care of ourselves. We accept that living at 1% is what makes "good moms." And it doesn't help that survival mode is celebrated and that any mom who dares to thrive is a selfish bitch.

Yet a generation before mine got us out of the house, if we chose. Sadly, society didn't adapt quickly enough to distribute the household workload evenly between two partners. No, working moms have no fewer expectations in the home now than anytime before. They just have nanny schedules to manage on top of it all.

The damage is so deep and so blanketed that an entire generation of moms are drowning, trying to get through it, and we are unconsciously passing the same demented blueprint on to our children—to our daughters and our sons—to expect the same in their future families and do nothing. Ensuring the desperation continues to the next generation.

It's time to end it all. We demand change. We demand it of ourselves. Because we alone can bring it. We don't need permission. We need a mass rebellion. That starts one woman at a time.

One night, scrolling through social media, I came across a post credited to @mommycusses, and it hit home:

"What some people don't understand is that she's living on 1%.

Nobody is feeding her.

No one takes care of her when she's sick.

Nobody is asking her what she needs.

No one is recharging her battery.

And she force stops.

She stops taking care of herself.

She yells.

She shuts down and gets side-eyed for it.

Plug her the fuck in. The moms are not okay."

I was not okay. Not remotely. Not in my soul. Not in my mind. Not in my body. Nowhere was I fine. I mean, I wasn't okay back with one kid and one business. How the hell I managed to survive 2020 with two kids, two businesses, and a pandemic is unfathomable.

I wanted some kind of confirmation I was on the right path. I sought honesty and a way to genuinely enjoy motherhood. I meditated on that. I hiked thinking about it. I listened to my heart. And that started to bring me back to sanity. But outside that sacred time. I didn't feel safe to share how it really was for me. I wasn't safe from women's judgment, from their gossip, and from social disappointment, and the person I was least safe from was myself.

My self-betrayal ran deep. That social expectation became my own, and it was a cruel taskmaster. After years of torturing myself with the private guilt and shame of not being good enough, while being praised externally by everyone else for "doing it all," I was deeply angry.

I took that anger to meditation. I walked with that anger up mountains, and I cried out that anger next to rivers, letting my tears fall into the currents. I practiced breathwork and breathed deeply into my pain, releasing it back out of my body, and when I finally saw it and named it, that's when the healing began.

The two hours ended up making enough space in my life to sort through the expectations, remember the painful lessons, and chart a way forward to bring me the boundaries I needed. I showed up many days and wandered and wondered about motherhood and what I didn't want to hold onto any longer.

SIX MONTHS TAKING TWO:
Strollers in the Crosswalk

I sat there at a red light, remembering how a couple months before simply hitting a red light would have sent my infant son into panicked screams. I think I'm permanently scarred for life. But there I was sitting at a red light, in the middle of the day, no kids and listening to an amazing song.

It was a good day.

And that's when I spotted them. I'd just come back from my two hours and was driving back across town to start my workday when I saw the double stroller and two curly topped heads peaking out, pointing at the fire station across the street, right next to where I was waiting for the light to turn green.

My heart sank. It's one thing to know your kids are with a nanny. It's another to watch the nanny enjoy time with your kids. Time you choose not to be with them.

Fuck. And just like that, I felt guilty again.

When would this end?!?

Twenty minutes ago, on my hike, I had told myself how proud I was of myself for getting out of the house, spending time in nature, and sorting my feelings.

But now that familiar doubt returned. Was I doing what was best for my family?

YES! A small desperate voice inside pipped up.

Yes, don't listen to that guilt. You're breaking a cycle. You're role modeling a new way to be emotionally healthy. This matters. Keep going.

I inhaled just as the light turned green. I turned, evading recognition and reminded myself, it's okay. I'll be okay.

SEVEN MONTHS TAKING TWO:
The Infamous Adult Tantrum Starring Yours Truly

It was what we as parents call the "witching hour." Not entirely sure why that is or why it still persists, but suffice to say, it's that fateful time of night where everyone is exhausted and it's right before dinner and bedtime.

And I found myself staring into the defiant angry eyes of a 4year-old standing in righteous judgement against her little brother ripping up her sacred new drawing of a rainbow and unicorn. In a tornado of vengeance, she had descended on her brother in a string of verbal and physical attacks, and he was fighting back, bless him.

Thank God I'd had my two hours that day because I surprised myself with my saint-like patience and spa-like tone of voice. Nothing could phase me. But it alarmed me because even as the queen of calm in that moment, Kennedy wasn't calming down. She was screaming, sobbing and clinging to me, struggling to breathe.

And I had just tried on conscious parenting tip number 3 to no avail. I whispered to myself, "What should I do?"

That's when my mind flashed back to that not so flattering time when I threw an adult sized tantrum.

Let me share:

It was 1 o'clock on a Sunday. My phone had already dropped two calls, the screen had frozen twice on FaceTime, I'd run out of storage, and my emails had stopped syncing. I had urgent emails I couldn't access, and in the middle of a tense conversation, the phone froze. Leaving annoyed words hanging in the air, I could feel the familiar mix of anger and panic rising inside of me. Bubbling up to the surface they came, threatening a parental version of a full-blown tantrum.

It all made sense. It was October, and the newest iPhone model had just been announced, and like clockwork, my phone was on the fritz. I swear every new iPhone launch, Apple decides it's time for you to upgrade and slowly starts to sabotage your phone on the daily until you crack or it does.

"Michael! I'm officially over it. I need a new phone. I'm going to head to the store now."

"Do you have insurance on it?"

"How would I know? You handled it last time."

I was beyond edgy. Every glance I sent around our new house was spewing eggshells … leaving no doubt how to navigate around me.

"Well I don't think we did. As long as it's not cracked, you should be fine."

"I need a new phone. I'm losing it."

"Okay, we can head to the Apple store later today."

"Let's go now."

As if on cue, one-and-a-half year old Kennedy toddled over to me, precariously holding my iPhone. Then it happened in slow motion. She toddled over my flip flops and lost her balance, my phone sliding free of her slippery grasp.

"NOOOOOOO!" I bellowed.

Smash! The entire screen shattered.

And something snapped inside me.

I picked up the phone, and in rage and panic, I threw it as hard as I could against the wall and then started to hyperventilate myself. I couldn't breathe. I couldn't think. What the hell was wrong with me? I looked at Michael, and his look of disapproval cut like a knife in my heart as he picked up a sobbing Kennedy. Protectively shielding her from her basket-case mom, he quietly walked outside and shut the front door.

Bitchy Brittany descended on me like a vulture. *That was Oscar worthy. Talk about a hot mess. What would your mother think about you if she saw that 32-year-old tantrum? Certainly Kennedy will be in therapy for years thanks to today.*

I still couldn't catch my breath. I was sobbing, trying to inhale, and my panicked thoughts swirled around me. *What the fuck is going on? Is this a panic attack?*

My central nervous system was spiraling out of control.

Calm down and breathe, came a loving warm voice from within.

I inhaled as best as I could. I felt like I was swimming upstream; my chest was so constricted. Finally, I got my breath to slow.

I was sitting on the floor in our bedroom, next to my full-sized dressing mirror.

I made eye contact with my reflection and didn't recognize myself. I was a monster, and a mom.

A monster mom. The very thing I swore I wouldn't become. I didn't want my daughter to grow up with an emotionally unstable mother. What had just happened?

I covered my face in my hands in shame and sobbed. It didn't make sense. It was just a stupid iPhone. Why had I reacted like that?

Because you're hell bent to have it all, and you insist on working too much. Look at you. Is this the picture of a model mother? Piped up Bitchy Brittany.

No, it wasn't. Twenty minutes later I apologized to Michael and Kennedy.

I'd just had a meltdown as a mom. Melt down or panic attack? The later.

Okay, so in that moment, with Kennedy losing it over a ruined art project, I realized she didn't know how to regulate her highly sensitive central nervous system, and she needed my help.

And I remembered that story about the iPhone and my panic attack. And I remembered all the Wim Hof breath work I'd been doing during my two hours.

So I held her and looked her in the eyes and said, "Kens, will you breathe with me? When I feel upset like this it helps me to breathe." She looked up at me with a look that told me how grateful she was to be "seen," and we hugged, and I talked her through deep breathing.

It worked. And it reminded me of the power of building skills to regulate emotions during my two hours and how much of an asset it is as a mother.

EIGHT MONTHS TAKING TWO:
My Breakthrough at the Nude Beach

Right about the eight-month mark, I started to shake loose a little with my two hours and got the inspired idea to become a "tourist" again in my town and use some of my time to explore beautiful places outside.

I decided to head to Pirate's Cove. If you were local, you'd know it's the only private beach which was locally known to be the nude beach in town. It's got a salty reputation, and every now and then you'd pick up the local newspaper and hear about how some policeman went undercover and arrested someone who propositioned them.

So why the hell was I there?!? Because while others may be drawn to the "no need for clothes" vibe, I knew a secret. Well, a secret spot, and there's an old climbing rope that you can use to climb down the cliffs and sit out privately, watching waves crash into a glorious rock formation that looks like an elephant.

I loved solitude with a view, so I perched out there one morning watching the tide ebb and flow, and I just zoned out and then had an epiphany.

It just came to me.

A happy mom is better than an ever-present mom.

Woah! That hit like truth!

A happy mom is better than an ever-present mom. Yep. Every. Single. Time.

I started to journal and unpack my thoughts around this.

Here's what I wrote:

"It's quality over quantity. Will my kids remember how much time I spent around them or will they remember who I was when I was with them? The latter. This gives me the permission I need each day to justify taking time to be away from my family and work so I could return to me. I needed to pursue happiness and see it as a gift to my family. My two hours a day wasn't hurting them; it was teaching them how powerful a mother figure is in their lives when she knows who the fuck she is; she prioritizes her health and she shows up in her fullness and joy to be present with them.

I am a better mother for taking care of myself."

Damn! That felt good to write. I stared off into the marine layer starting to roll in, and a memory from the night before popped into my brain.

Yesterday I hadn't take my alone time first thing in the morning, and by the afternoon, I'd got myself all worked up about someone coming over to visit (so out of practice since the pandemic that it felt monumental), and Kennedy just looked up at me with her large blue eyes and said, "Mom, did you have your alone time today?"

Shit. Called out.

"No, I didn't," I said.

"Why don't you do it now so you can be happy?"

And I felt so proud. I didn't feel any mom guilt at that moment. I teared up and smiled. Because as a mom, the ultimate judge of our parenting isn't our mothers, our sisters, or our friends. It's ourselves and our own children. My daughter knows the power two hours a day has. It always made me happier, and she wanted that for me. I'd taught her that, and she knew it so well. She'd often ask for her own alone time because she loved being alone too.

NINE MONTHS TAKING TWO:
Learning To Mother Myself

I think if someone were to tell me I'd embrace reparenting myself a year ago, I would have laughed in their face. Re-parent myself? I'm 34 years old, thank you. The time for parenting is in my rearview mirror. I don't have time for that.

But during one of my two hours, I decided to see a healer. With no real agenda, other than to see why she was so well respected.

I was in a healing session, and the healer asked me to envision a mother figure who embodied all the qualities of a mother that I, as a child, would want from a mother. I breathed deeply, choking back tears almost instantly. The power of mother energy flooded over me.

Kind communicator

Compassionate

Nurturer of your spirit

Intuitive truth seeker

Cultivator of talents

Emotionally and physically reassuring

Consistent and reliable

Unconditional love

Gentle and strong

I was asked to visualize that pure mother energy coming into my heart and sitting with me. I broke down into tears. It was so beautiful, so loving, so safe.

I was encouraged to find that energy inside of myself, and to stop expecting anyone else in my life to show up like that for me, that I had it all inside of my soul, the God-given capabilities to be a mother to my own self as well as for my children. It was such a profound experience for me. I sobbed in that session. It touched me so deeply. To realize I could stop blaming and start healing myself, to believe that I had it in me and just needed to cultivate it.

Our potential as mothers is powerful—not just for our kids but as mothers to our own selves. I started to practice speaking to myself like a loving mother, not a nasty critic.

When I'm running late instead of saying:

"My god, Paden, you are so disrespectful of people's time," I could stop and think, "It's okay, Honey. You're doing your best and can honor them for their patience."

When I'd snap at my kids and watch them react to me like I was a monster, instead of saying, "You're a wreck. You're destroying your kids," I'd pause and say, "Woah, Paden, it's okay. You're safe. You're supported. You're loved. Take a breath. I'm so proud of you for catching yourself right now. This reaction isn't you. Pause, and try again to express what you're really wanting to express."

When I'd make a witty jab at Michael and feel that familiar pang of guilt when I see the look he gave me, instead of saying, "God, he must hate you right now. You're such a dirtbag for saying that," I'd say, "Woah, Paden, take a deep breath. Recenter yourself. It's okay to feel upset. How can you communicate the truth of what you mean with love? Try again, my love."

I took that concept and idea to meditation, on my walks, and kept it with me when I danced. I consciously practiced stepping in as a mother to my own soul. I saved some of my energy for myself, not just the leftovers at the end of a weary day. I saved some of my best energy for myself, and it was one of the most powerful takeaways of my two hours.

When you step away from the mayhem, the chaos, and the pressure we place on moms, and we look into the healing a conscious, loving mother can bring to this world, it's staggering. It's not something I feel guilt about. I feel inspired to tap into this abundant gift and to share it with myself and my kids.

It was my way back to self-love. When I stopped beating myself up as a critic and stepped in as the loving, nurturing mother, I felt safe in my body for the first time. I was not at war inside. I was my advocate, my protector, my soul's caretaker, and someone who built me up.

Motherhood unlocks the potential for powerful gifts, gifts I explored and pondered as I spent my time alone daily.

ELEVEN MONTHS TAKING TWO:
Listening to the Whispers of My Inner Wise Woman

In the silence of my two hours, I got insight about how to move forward wisely. Out of the stillness, I found encouragement for everything I had done well. I also got profound answers in space.

The warm, loving voice inside started to teach me things like …

Your kids need you home even more. You need to cut back your work schedule to 20 hours a week, not the 35 you've been doing.

Your daughter doesn't feel safe with her preschool teacher. It's good for her to be home with her brother the next eight months. Pull her out.

Put your phone down during bath time. Use this time to connect.

Take your kids out each week for a special Mommy Date so they feel seen, prioritized, and cared for.

Alternate which parent comes home first so Michael can take them on fun playdates, and you can work later one some days without guilt.

Instead of resenting Jackson for his early wake up time, turn it into a special date and enjoy time with just him.

Stop sleep training the kids at bedtime. It's okay for them to need you to lay down next to them for them to fall asleep.

Come home at 2:30 pm and take them out in nature. It will restore all of your souls and start teaching them to seek solace in nature. Don't just use your time at home with them to hustle them around to appointments, errands, or chores. Play and explore with them.

Share the hard things on social media so other mothers don't feel so alone. Don't fear the judgment from others. Use your voice to bring connection to other mothers struggling like you.

On the weekends, take your two hours first thing in the morning. Let Michael wake up with the kids, enjoy some coffee and cartoons with them, and your absence will be noticed less.

And every time I listened, my family responded so much better to me. And magically, I felt less guilt, and I could see how valuable taking this time was for me. Developing sensitivity to my own maternal instincts and intuition allowed me to stop caring what social expectations were handed down to me. It allowed me the confidence to chart my own course and see the peace and happiness that it brought my family.

CONCLUSION

Making space to think and consider is so damned powerful, especially as mothers. We spend so much time learning about pregnancy, how to give birth, and very little time on learning how to keep an infant alive for the first six weeks. And we somehow skip the shift to becoming a mother entirely, as if it's supposed to be so natural that we'll find our way.

And so often we lose ourselves in motherhood, far deeper and more profoundly than we ever lost ourselves to please a boss or significant other.

But the gift I received through the journey of my two hours a day was that I could unpack the rage I'd buried within me and make peace with it.

Two hours started off as a way to heal physically from signs of chronic stress. I had never intended to use it to help alleviate me from the pressures of motherhood.

But the journey taught me that we are all healers. As our skin has the ability to heal a cut, we can heal emotionally and mentally too, but we have to slow the fuck down so we can recognize what needs to be healed, and we have to learn to listen to the silence and pick up the messages meant for us.

What I know about Motherhood is that it's ever changing. Just as soon as I get used to one thing, another thing pops up. It's like a giant game of Hungry Hippo. You're always ready for something else to troubleshoot or a guilty thought to pop up for a eighty-ninth time.

I've come to expect Mom guilt to surge back into my awareness because I'm still undoing much of the social expectations around what being a good mother looks like, and I'd be lying if mom guilt still didn't land a few punches, particularly when someone close to me puts their voice to an ugly judgment.

As I consider Motherhood, here's what I'm learning how to integrate into my life:

I am trying on new ways to bring magic to my kids. Not in the insane and ever so popular way of trying to make so much damn magic for your kids that every day feels like it's Elf on the Shelf time, but in ways that foster magic. Like the time my kids discovered bean pods at a park, saved all the beans and then planted them in our front yard, and later that night, after they went to bed, we planted 2 foot tall "beanstalks" for them to wake up to. That reaction was magic.

Or when I desire to go into nature and no one wants to join me, to turn it into a full on reenactment of my son's favorite book, "Going on a Bear Hunt," and we sing the song along the way at every new obstacle in our path. Those are the memories I am more present for, and those are the times I savor.

I am care-fronting my friends who make comments about how working moms of little kids are hurting their development. I have decided that sharing opinions like that aren't how I experience love and support, and I desire to feel loved and supported by my inner circle. It's now an agreement I have with myself that to be a part of my inner circle, I need to feel respected and valued, even if our choices and beliefs are different.

I am giving myself permission to ask for help when I am overstimulated and not showing up the way I want to. I believe there will never be a village of support for moms unless moms start asking for help and being willing to express what's hard to other moms. So I'm practicing asking other moms for help. I also ask the kids to play for a minute while I step away to collect myself, and I anticipate better when I need alone time to recalibrate my nervous system.

chapter 9
SHOTS BEFORE SEX

"If and when you meet someone who catches your eye, hold his gaze. Then walk up behind him, trace a single finger down his back. And if he follows you into a dark corner of the bar, it's meant to be."
—Moira, *Schitt's Creek*

WEEK 1 TAKING TWO:
She's Back!

It was 1 o'clock on a Tuesday. What the fuck was going on? I was so damned horny, I kept checking Michael's schedule to see if he had a break for a booty call.

Who am I? What the hell is going on? This felt reckless and awesome. We'd had sex every day the last week, and I still wanted more.

So here's the thing. Of all the healing paths my two hours led me on, sex was one of the first major breakthroughs. Just taking two hours a day for myself had reduced my stress load so dramatically, I got the space to discover my own wants and desires. Which led me to sex, something that had felt like a "nice to have" versus a "need" for too long.

After having my second kid, who came out hating sleep, going through post-partum depression, struggling to keep up with a needy toddler, juggling, running a household and a businesses, it was no surprise that sex was one of the furthest things from my mind. I didn't want to be touched by anyone. I wanted to sleep. It wasn't that I didn't crave connection. I was just too damn tired and depleted to put any effort into it. (And deep down I didn't want one more person wanting something from me.)

I'd left Michael hanging more than I'd like to admit. For the previous couple of years, my libido had been keeping pace with my mommy brain. It had only been seven days since I started taking two hours a day, and it seemed like my sex drive instantly returned. I felt so energized, so happy to be playing again in my life and focusing on my well-being that my libido rose like a phoenix from the ashes. Oh my god… is this what happens when you're a nympho? Have we actually crossed over into clinical? I flipped my script overnight and had turned into a sex machine. Michael joked that if this was the only thing that came out of taking two hours a day, "you have my full support."

Taking two hours daily had given me back a sense of self that allowed me to step into feeling sexy again and wanting sex. At first, I thought it was a side effect of a woman finally showing up for her needs and, in doing so, reawakening her sex drive, but based on the amount of real estate this topic takes up in this book, you can guess there's a far deeper story here than just a tired mom wanting more sex. And you'd be right. As the months progressed with me taking time daily, I dove into shadows and memories that cracked me wide open and brought me to far greater healing than I could have anticipated.

WEEK 3 TAKING TWO:
Are ALL Spiritual Teachers Sex Gurus?

I jumped into my car, wondering yet again, "What should I do today?"

I saw the beautiful blue sky and sunshine and felt pulled to go on a hike, somewhere near the ocean. Thank God it's only an eight-minute drive.

Like most days, I decided to use the time during the drive to learn something, so I jumped back into a podcast I'd only heard half of earlier that morning when I was juggling kids, switching between the cartoons they wanted to watch, applying eyeliner, and flipping eggs.

It was an Aubrey Marcus podcast featuring Layla Martin. And without remembering a shred of context, here's what I heard:

"When you're talking about unwinding your performative self, it gets back to trusting yourself and trusting your bodily sensations and pleasure…" Layla Martin shared. What? What was this podcast even about? The title was Sexual Healing. How had I clicked on that?

Well, it was one enlightening eight-minute car ride.

I was well aware that the healing journey I was on was physical AND soulful. For whatever reason, my brain had never considered sexuality as the obvious nexus of my physical and spiritual roads—like, never in a million years.

I felt flustered. I got to the trailhead and turned off the podcast. At week three, I'd learned that if I kept listening, I'd just be consuming more information and miss out on being myself, relaxed and free.

I started out on the path with a simple curiosity, "Are all spiritual gurus highly sexual?"

Uh, duh, Paden. We're all sexual beings.

I KNEW that in theory, but I grew up in a predominantly Christian community, where the only time a pastor's sexuality was up for public discussion was if they'd cheated on their wife, were publicly confessing their crimes … OR they'd been discovered to be some kind of pervert, and that put their name in the local or national headlines. I was not used to spiritual leaders talking about their relationships to their penises publicly, much less women speaking about their pussies casually. And honestly, it made me squeamish.

Maybe I was a prude.

But this podcast got me thinking. I couldn't ignore these things:

1. It made sense that sex was designed to be sacred (as a product of purity culture, as I'd been taught).
2. I had grown up believing that emotions and feelings were not to be trusted. Only the cognitive mind or the Bible could be trusted. So maybe I had disconnected from my body.
3. I had always known I was a deeply sexual person, with no idea on how to harness it.
4. Even in the last three weeks, just from taking time away from my demanding life, I'd seen my libido return. Was that just because I had a break from my stress, or was it connected to my larger healing?

If listening to a bit of a podcast got me to connect the dots, it was clear my sexuality was a healing exploration I was going on. Great, so much for lighted heartedness and fun for two hours, I was diving into some more deep territory. I reminded myself, this was about healing. Nothing was off limits if it promised a path to healing. So I stepped into using the two hours to unpack what the fuck had gone wrong with my sexuality.

6 WEEKS TAKING TWO:
That Damn Duke

The catalyst was Netflix. Well, Bridgerton, actually. Yes, it was sexy, and I wanted to have more sex after watching that show, like the millions of us that were glued to that series when it came out. But it hit me in a different way. That damned show sent me off into my two hours thinking about how I had first discovered sexuality and what I had been taught about it. It's only for marriage.

Good girls wait.

Do everything you can to save even your first kiss for the altar.

The right man won't push you, won't try anything with you. If he does, he's selfish and not a good life partner. And remember, finding your life partner is the ultimate goal. Until you do that, sex is not for you.

I thought about society's double standard for men. Maybe the conservative standard was the same for both genders, but society put a lot of pressure on men to be experienced, and made it okay that they were. I wrestled with how this had impacted me personally and how I'd watch it impact my friends. I had seen Bridgerton's Daphne as "sexually repressed." I related to her and all the pressure she was under. Was I repressed like that, I wondered.

I didn't like that word, much less the thought. I shut down that line of thinking and decided to jump to a guided meditation instead.

2 MONTHS TAKING TWO:
Sand and Shots

I sat there, toes wiggling in the sand like my two-year-old had done earlier in the week. I let the sunlight bathe my face, probably making way for more freckles … or, God forbid, sun spots.

I was processing the mind-body disconnection I was more than suspecting I had. The rhythmic sound of the waves hitting the shore lulled me into my memories, and out of no where I recalled a therapy session:

"Do you think it ever hurts Michael's feelings?"

"What?"

"Your habit of taking two shots before having sex?"

Ew, rude.

I honestly hadn't ever considered it. Don't all men just want their good little Christian wives to shed their prudish facades and let loose behind closed doors?

The only way I'd been able to do that, and enjoy sex, was if I pounded back one or more shots to help me get out of my head. (I offered him one while I was at it.) It was the best way I'd figured out to stop being so in my head during sex, but I didn't want to tell my therapist that.

"No, he doesn't seem to mind," I answered, like I didn't care.

"Have you ever asked him?" I was beyond offended now, and my Irish was starting to show.

"I don't have to ask him," I said, defensive as hell, as if I didn't know my own husband. "Sex is better for us both when I'm relaxed."

"I don't doubt it," she said. "Do you ever wonder why you need alcohol to let down your guard?"

The nerve! I couldn't believe I was paying someone to sit there and insult me. But, of course, I hadn't thought much about why I needed alcohol. Why would I question something that seemed to help me?

I thought this was normal. Doesn't every housewife in America try to get tipsy for porn-like sex with their partner of x years? I was aware that, statistically, I was competing with 18-year-olds with baby-skin vaginas and double-D boob jobs. So, yeah, I'd drink one or two shots first.

I knew what she was implying though, that I was repressed and had to resort to using substances to help me get past my fears and inability to naturally connect to my body during sex.

But I wasn't ready to talk about that. I didn't want to go into why that was happening. I mentally shut down and ended the session early, muttering something about having to pick up the kids.

But the therapist's questions nagged me. Why did I need alcohol to feel sexy? Maybe it was the word "need" next to the word "alcohol" that shook me up. Did I have a drinking problem or just a getting-comfortable-during-sex problem? Shit.

Maybe I was self-medicating to cover up how hard it was for me to connect to pleasure. I didn't like the idea that I was putting a Band-Aid over a gaping wound. I started to obsessively think about whether the therapist was right about Michael too.

Was I offending Michael? Was my drinking making him feel like he wasn't naturally sexy enough to turn me on? Did I even have a wild side that I was capable of accessing without "help?" Or was I just acting like it to fulfill a fantasy? I panicked. Michael didn't seem to "need" it, although he occasionally had a shot with me. He knew I got turned on by kisses laced with lingering scotch.

Was I really the one who needed it? I mean, if there was a catalog of men with Michael in it, I'd still pick him. He just gets hotter with age. It wasn't about him. It was me. When did I ever feel sexy? I mean, there was always the sexy test for the younger, unmarried me. I got dressed up and walked through a bar and counted how many gazes I'd drawn, but when I was alone with my husband, did I feel uninhibited? Did I feel wild and beautiful? Untamed? Sometimes, but it was hard to predict, unless I threw back a shot of scotch. That always worked.

That's all I needed, and then I became someone different, confident to be naked in the light, watching myself in the full length mirror next to our bed, free to follow my fantasies without judging them as dirty. The scotch just took off the edge. And it was easy, easier than dealing with what was really going on. With alcohol, I could be wild, adventurous, and sexy. I liked her better, and I didn't know how to awaken her without those shots of scotch.

Where had that memory come from? I didn't like thinking about that conversation, even now on a soul exploration. It really fucked with my confidence.

I walked back up to the staircase leading up the cliffside back to the parking lot, consumed with my feelings on the subject. I was angry all over again. How dare someone (even from my past) add one more thing for me to feel bad about. My cheeks burned because I knew there was truth to it, truth I hadn't wanted to hear then, and I wasn't sure I was ready to now.

I got to my car and saw three texts from the office and pushed the continuation of this thinking away. I had to start my work day, and I mentally shifted back into Boss mode.

3 MONTHS TAKING TWO:
The Defense Calls the Infamous Banana Incident

I sat up on top of one of the Seven Sisters, the seven peaks in our county that tower over the small towns. The wind was gentle, the sunlight warm and inviting, and the birds were all happily singing, flying from bush to bush all around me. I was aware of the dissonance in the scene. I was annoyed with the word "repressed," so of course, I started to obsess about how unrepressed I really was, trying to win an internal debate about a topic I was awkward about.

That's when I remembered the Christmas Banana story.

Okay, so were you that kid who gave handwritten coupons for Christmas? You know, "Good for One Massage" or "Good for One Back Scratch?" I grew up using those because every Christmas Eve, I'd look at all the presents I had to wrap for my siblings and parents, and it never seemed like enough, so I'd throw in some good last minute additions, to ensure they loved my presents, and it was a pretty good deal too, because like most business owners figure out, 25 percent of the time people don't even remember they have gift cards and never step up to claim them.

Well, some habits from childhood carry into adulthood. Christmas 2019, I was faced with an empty stocking for my husband. (I know what you're thinking, why the hell do we still give ourselves stockings as adults? Because as Marie Kondo says, "It sparks joy.") I had a couple of the basics: toothpaste, socks, and deodorant, but I pride myself on being an intuitive gift giver. I had found some amazing gifts, but with sadness in my heart, I had to forego buying them because, plain and simple, that year I didn't have any money to spend. We were launching a new business and had just put every penny we had saved up of our personal money into the launch. It was exciting and risky, but it didn't change the fact that the max I could justify spending on Michael was $30. In moments when money is tight, I tend to get macro. "What are their love languages?" "What have I done in the past as an act of service that they appreciated?" Michael's main love language is Physical Touch, so I instantly went to sex, and because you can't fill a stocking with sex, I started to think about coupons.

How corny would it be if I created coupons for sexual experiences, I wondered? Pretty fucking corny, but I kinda roll with corny. My mind wandered instantly to that time when I convinced my entire group of mom friends to try having sex once per day for a month, just to break us all out of reverting to the same tired positions that exhausted parents with multiple kids end up settling for. It felt inspired.

I felt damned proud of myself for that one.

I wondered if I still had the list on my shared notes. Yep, there it was, the full list. I scrolled through the list of different themes for each day of the month and remembered something interesting from that night—no one wanted to give oral sex. (Or you know, blow jobs, head, "going down on", you get it). Zero.

Does that surprise you? A group of a dozen moms drinking wine, laughing like virgins at the title "whip nip night," but totally shooting down anything having to do with oral sex. So we kept it more granola with nights like sex in the shower, sex with the lights on, sex in a new room in the house, and other ideas to pull us out of having default sex in the dark.

But I can't tell you how many of my mom friends get squeamish around the topic of oral sex. They feel like they're acting like porn stars, which in those circles is NOT a good thing.

It feels dirty.

It's just gross.

It tastes bad.

Did he honestly want me to swallow it?

That shit's for single girls who can't have sex before marriage. Why would I do it now?

At that time, I thought I was good at sex, but oral sex? What about some kind of coupon about blow jobs? Doubt crowded in. Was I even good at blow jobs? I didn't share most of the sentiments of my friends, but I was getting pretty lazy in my foreplay game, so I Googled something that would have made my friends blush: "How to give a good blow job." I got slightly paranoid that the government was watching me search for this or that that simple search would trigger porn advertisements and crash my computer, but thankfully none of that happened, that I know of.

What did happen was I found an online $30 ebook to teach women how to give the best blow jobs. I looked past the blatant sexist language and reassurances that this course would help you keep your man from breaking up with you and ditching you for another woman, but I'm a learner at heart, so I kept reading because outside of giving blow jobs to every boyfriend I had since high school, what real proof did I have that I had any skills? I mean, I had a warm mouth. Wasn't that all that was needed? Probably not.

So as creepy and weird as it felt to buy an ebook, probably written by some 19-year-old software engineer with acne whose copywriting and hacking skills had helped him build this sales funnel to teach insecure wives how to give a better blow job, I was on the fence about how legit this ebook was. But it was two days before Christmas. What finally sealed the deal was my grand idea of what to put in his stocking to unveil my gift.

As soon as the idea struck me, I had to do it. It was just too good.

Christmas morning, Michael opened his stocking and pulled out a banana. He gave me a look like "WTF is this doing in my stocking, gross." Then he read it and he laughed. "2020: the year I master the art of a damn good blow job and will need lots of practice."

To this day he still says it was one of my very best presents.

Oh, 2020, the year I felt like I was sexually open, adventurous, and in complete denial to how sexually repressed I really was. I mean, I gave the man a damned banana and studied porn videos to improve my BJ game. Repressed? Ha!

There you have it! My evidence. How could someone repressed do either of those things?

I was agitated still. So I turned on my Spotify playlist "Soul Music" and let the music carry me into a better mental place for the remaining hour of my two hours.

5 MONTHS TAKING TWO:
Okay, I Admit It. I'm Repressed.

I would never have identified with the concept of repression until I went out to dinner with one of my best friends who grew up in Italy, and we started to share about our upbringings.

Our conversation flowed easily, like the wine in our glasses. We covered my religious upbringing, her agnostic upbringing, our relationships with our parents, my relationship with my husband, her relationship with her ex-husband. And then the conversation turned to sex. She was shocked that I hadn't had sex until I was 21 and had only had a couple partners. I was equally shocked by the openness in her upbringing. We came from such different backgrounds and had both been introduced to sexuality in polar opposite ways. I remember she raised her eyebrows and said, "This is honestly the most open conversation I've had about sex with an American. What's with you all? In Italy we talk about sex all the time, and it's not a big deal." I knew what she meant. The women I knew seemed to just know we don't talk about sex specifically and only mention it openly if it's in admiration of our husbands or to assure everyone you were "good to go" in that department.

"Check the box, Katie is, in fact, still having sex. Moving along ... "

All joking aside, my friend Sara and I launched into a full discussion about what it was like for her growing up in Italy, where sex is a coming-of-age rite of passage. It's something you learn how to do early and enjoy for life. It's not as big of a deal. Meanwhile, she was horrified to learn how I'd grown up in relation to sex. Leaving that conversation, I was willing to admit that I was likely more in the repressed camp than in the expressed camp.

I still didn't like the way that sounded, so one morning in the parking lot outside of the trailhead where I was planning to hike, I Googled sexual repression.. I still liked sex. How could I be repressed? I read the Google generated list and instantly got triggered.

- Not achieving an internal orgasm
- Harshly judging others for their sexual preferences or tastes
- Being disassociated from your body's pleasure and hyper-focused on your partners' sexual satisfaction
- Faking being in the mood and being performative in sex (possibly why 60% of us admit to faking orgasms)
- Avoiding masturbating, or feeling guilty after, like you've "cheated" on your partner
- Being self-conscious when naked or in lingerie
- Having wild sex dreams where your partner is not the person you're having sex with
- The inability to ask for help or what you want (not just about sex)
- Closet lover of erotica or addicted to reading graphic romance novels, but you get really uncomfortable watching a sex scene with anyone. The fake prude game.
- You have a vibrator buried in your underwear drawer and would be mortified if anyone found it
- Intolerant of any sexual expression
- Label certain sex acts as bad or dirty
- And of course, the one I began with, taking shots before sex to relax

I saw myself in so much of the list and hated it. I may as well have been the poster child for this. So if you identify with any of the above list, know that you're not alone. Sure, I could feel pleasure, but never without battling my mind to fucking relax or experiencing some kind of insecurity. Sex was great, but somehow it was always complicated.

I got out of the car and started to hike like I was on some kind of mission. Not at all the free-spirited woman I wanted to become.

I was processing what I'd just read. Three miles later, here's what I came back with.

Sexual repression doesn't happen overnight. It's not one persons' fault. It's fueled by cautionary stories, thinly-veiled judgments, institutional rule-making, and by witnessing how we punish sexually expressive women, compared to how we praise the good girls. We are survivors in nature, particularly when we were not at the top of the food chain. Something most of us women learned early on. So we adapted. It's handed down through so many channels and in so many ways. The message is surprisingly unified:

If you ignore, push down, and stifle any and all sexual urges or expressions before marriage, somehow you'll preserve the most pure, sacred part of you. And then you'll get married and embark on a hot and magical journey with your spouse. Together you'll be pure, unjaded and get to unwrap the gift of sexuality together. It'll be 1000% better and more sacred because you will be pure.

And like so many good Christian girls, I bought into that. Believing it led me deep into sexual repression as a teenager, and I had all sorts of side effects as a grown-ass married woman. I spent many of my two-hour time blocks meditating on my relationship to sex and my body. I found places I was super self-conscious and needed healing around. I started to dance on my hikes. I'd just put on some music and listen and move with the music. Being in my body like that started to show me all the places in my body I was stuck. It came up in funny ways too, like being worried someone would come around the corner and see me dancing seductively on the side of a mountain. Why did I even care? But I did.

Yet I kept dancing. I kept getting into my body and practicing connecting to my sexuality again. Through dance. Just me. Dancing for me. Not for anyone else. There was no male gaze. There was no one to seduce but myself. Movement heals. And trauma is stored so often in the body. For me, dancing was profoundly healing, and after, I'd think. I pieced together why I felt so disconnected from my body to begin with, and as unpopular a sentiment as this is, I don't know how you can grow up in a conservative religious background without some warped views of sex and sexuality that still linger.

In fact, I believe it was Sigmund Freud who said that sexual repression is the chief psychological problem we face in society. So, welcome to having THAT conversation with me. (Bet you didn't think we were going here.) I am of the opinion that too many of us have an archaic definition of what sexual suppression is, and I believe this deserves a far broader discussion. Suppression impacts most of us in some way. We tend to think of sexual repression as:

- Reluctance to act on your sexual desires
- Sex-related fear or anxiety
- Guilt associated with sexual desires
- Harsh self-judgment of your sexual fantasies or your partners'

But Google put out a far more common and easy to overlook list.

Experiencing your sexuality by first trying to control and suppress it is more than being scared to have sex, or not enjoying sex. I relate that to the days when we'd hear someone was having mental health issues and instantly jump to the assumption that the person in question was suicidal or dealing with severe panic attacks. We now know that mental health is something we all grapple with to varying degrees. That's how I see sexual repression. It's more nuanced.

I heard a small inner voice break through the judgment swirling in my brain. *It's okay to feel this way. You're doing a brave thing by looking into this.* Keep going. There is more here to uncover.

SEVEN MONTHS TAKING TWO:
Ode to the Sexually Repressed Good Girls

One day I felt so bogged down with my confusion around sex and how to heal from repression that instead of going on a hike, I decided to journal my feelings. I've always felt at home with words, so I thought, perhaps, the way out of repression is actually expression.

I sat there getting my flywheel going before I journaled. I thought about sex being great, but also being so mental for me. I was always in my head, and without alcohol to help me, how could I get to a place of being present? There had to be a way to release this.

My inner truth spoke: *Give yourself permission to see what happened to you. See yourself. See the journey you have been on.*

But others have it worse.

Yes, but that doesn't change that trauma is trauma.

I closed my eyes and went back into the archives.

And when I did that, it cracked me wide open.

I am convinced that each of us have stories, like the kind I'm about to share with you. Stories that are painful, shame-inducing, or even triggering, but if we don't process the pain, we can't let it go.

There is no way to fully capture the voice of sexual repression from an inclusive lens. This is my experience, the only one I can really speak to, and I speak as a heterosexual married white woman. My life was and still is dripping with privilege, and I acknowledge that the topic of sexual repression goes far deeper for many people.

For me, that was through gradual courageous reconsidering that I did during the two hours that I was able to really understand where all this came from. So I'm sharing with you my journaling about what experiences I walked through that led me to discovering why my sexual repression was actually trying to protect me from more pain.

Ode to the Sexually Repressed Good Girls

Here's to the good girl, praised as a good listener, for following direction, anticipating everyone else's needs first, catering to the expectations of those around her, selfless to the point of having no individual desires or dreams.

The 5-year-old girl, told her body is sacred, shamed for discovering her clitoris during nap-time, taught that her body is a temple... but not for her. Enjoying it herself was a sin, dirty, that her body's pleasure should be saved for another, meaning, her future husband.

To the private school girl, measuring the length of her skirts so she wouldn't be publicly slut shamed, blamed for seducing her horny male peers with her revealing attire—the only self-control being judged was hers—warned that such actions lead to rape and sexual abuse, the results of not following society's rules.

To the girl whose true sex education came at an 8th grade sleep over featuring American Pie and got confused about what a pie had to do with sexual awakening.

To the girl who spent years stuffing down her natural urges, not exploring pleasure in any form, made to believe her inherent worth was tied to how "innocent" she was, the price of being good marriage material and attracting a Godly man.

To the good girl who tried and failed, finding other less offensive orifices to fill with her boyfriend. In an effort to keep their interest, she got the thrill of rebellion, never forgetting that keeping those hymens intact was really what kept you pure and whole, the only thing truly off limits.

To the good girl, who watched the boys she dreamed of and drooled over pick girls more in touch with their sexuality, the "bad girls," who seemed to have sexual power and were the most desired—making them targets of the good girls' gossip.

To the girl clutching her car keys between her fingers, as she walks nervously to her car, believing rapists are waiting for her to make the wrong move, always painfully aware of being just minutes away from becoming a statistic.

To the girl who went on her first business trip, got introduced to a top industry executive, only to be sexually assaulted by a powerful, perverted old man in plain sight, not an eyebrow raised, not even by his wife.

To the girl who had a panic attack at a networking event and took a cab ride to an unknown part of a big city to get drunk at a bar for the sole purpose of being hit on by men her own age, so desperate to feel in control and not even questioning that she'd be objectified no matter where she went.

To the good girl who sat up in bed at night worried about her emotionally distant boyfriend and decided to have sex to save their relationship.

To the good girl who had sex for the first time in a dirty college bedroom, hiding under the covers, caught in a confusing mix of excitement and shame, trying not to make a sound in case the religious roommates heard.

To the good girl who found herself being aggressively stripped naked and abused regardless of the word "stop" and then was laughed at for not being "into it," shamed for not wanting to reenact something that left her feeling dirty and degraded.

To the good girl whose boyfriend couldn't get a hard on no matter how much foreplay or how many new positions she tried, she believed it was all her fault, thought she wasn't sexy enough. She lacked experience after all, and nothing he wanted came naturally to her.

To the girl who found the guts to ask her boyfriend why he couldn't cum, and felt horrified when he admitted to jacking off three times a day to airbrushed, curvy porn stars rather than having sex with her and her skinny body.

To the good girl who discovered the past boyfriend, the one she'd wanted to marry, was a porn addict and didn't care to change. Her pretty little heart and sexual identity broke that day.

To the sexually repressed, underexpressed, unsacred girl still hoping marriage would finally give her a safe place to explore a thing called pleasure ... but could only manage to calm her anxiety with a couple shots.

To the good girl, the pretty girl, the sexually traumatized and still repressed girl.

To the girl I know so well. We all know her so well—because she is all of us.

I closed my journal and stopped writing. Just thinking all of this through in one sitting was so overwhelming for me. My emotions quickly rose in my throat, and tears welled into my eyes. I broke down and sobbed. Two hours of ugly crying under a tree, not 100 feet from the trailhead. I could barely make it off the path before the tears hit. Feeling the refreshed pain and the shame wash over me. Every emotional scar was visible to me, and it broke me that day.

And to anyone whose experience makes mine pale in comparison, my heart goes out to you. I cannot fathom the depth of that pain because my own consumed me.

Pain carries power with it. That day it ushered in a great purging of all my stored up anger, fear, shame and sadness and was, itself, one of the most impactful two hours I spent that whole year and a half. I gave myself permission to let all the feelings out, to let them flow through my veins unchecked, unrestrained, leaving me feeling tired but somehow stronger and more whole.

Sex and not feeling free to express sexuality carried so much deep shame for me. I was in a dysfunctional relationship with my sexuality, yet I recognized it held the power to heal a part of me, but I couldn't summon it without a stiff drink. That is, until I started spending two hours a day and finally confronted a lot of my sexual repression.

8 MONTHS TAKING TWO:
Owning My Pleasure

Studies show that stress is one of the biggest killers of libido. Simply taking two hours a day to be refreshed was significantly reducing my stress. I think the biggest reason couples' sex lives suffer is the strain of their demanding lives.

Infusing my busy life with two hours to jump off the hamster wheel and remember there was fun and that rest was available to me ... gave me back my libido.

Seriously.

I'd always been told that the sexual peak for men is 18 and for women its 35. Well, let me tell you, I was right on time. I couldn't get enough sex.

My increase in libido and subsequent deep dive into spirituality started to expose my vulnerabilities around sex and pleasure. As self-care is to personal development, sexuality is to spirituality. They are intricately woven together.

It's difficult to explore the world of spirituality without eventually discovering concepts like sacred union, sexually-open relationships, kundalini awakening, tantric sex magic or manifesting through orgasms.

These will come up. For example, one of my coaches during this time, Abbey Gibb, said it this way: "Your dreams won't come until you do."

Squirmy, much?

You should have seen my face in that group Zoom call. I blushed and looked confused, as if I hadn't heard her right the first time. Somehow, even in this mastermind of brilliant, badass CEO females, the subject of masturbation was coming up, and of course, I smiled, nodded along like I had the faintest idea of what she meant. I can count on one hand the women I have talked to about masturbation in my entire life. And here I was, a couple months into my spiritual awakening and masturbation was somehow connecting to a spiritual awakening.

In my exploration, I became very aware of several blocks I had to opening up more sexually. I was not tuned into my own sexual expression. Outside of sex with Michael, I didn't have a pleasure practice. I was feeling blocked creatively at work, and I knew it all was related.

The big epiphany I made regarding sexuality is that sexual energy is creator energy.

The same energy that helps you achieve orgasm brings your dreams to life, which meant sexuality was my connection to manifesting abilities and had to be released for me to step into the life I wanted to create.

I had to decide that being in touch with my body meant being in touch with pleasure, and when your time to get grounded, to manifest and explore spirituality, is in the middle of the work day … your journey will be solo. Which I needed more than anything. I didn't need anyone else to perform for. I didn't need to wonder if I was shaved, or if my body was in an attractive position.

I needed to be alone, on the top of a mountain, bathed in sunlight, finally figuring out how to experience pleasure on my own. Vibrator free. Not fantasizing in my mind. Instead, being turned on by myself. That may sound difficult to do, but if you do it, it's so damn freeing.

Growing up, I'd missed out on a very personal journey of discovering my sexuality as it unfolded and felt natural, but I reclaimed that one day, overlooking the ocean, on top of a hill, off the beaten path. I listened to a guided meditation called "kundalini awakening," and it was the first time I felt something change in my body during meditation. Energy shot through me from the base of my spine to my head.

The next day I went back to the same spot during my two hours, played good music and couldn't shake how damned sexy I felt, all by myself. That was new. No external validation needed. I was just turned on. So I masturbated right there in the sunlight on the side of a mountain overlooking the ocean, and in doing so, I liberated myself.

A part of me healed right then. I felt wild, free of inhibitions, and I hadn't had a sip of alcohol. For the first time, I felt the gift of my body. Its pleasure was for me and me alone. I felt something inside my mind change too. I released decades of sexual judgment.

9 MONTHS TAKING TWO:
Cleaning Up My Act Around Emasculation

Later that week I listened to an inspired video by Stefanos Sifandos, and he connected the dots for me between women who emasculate their man and their own self-care. It feels embarrassing to admit this, but given all we've been through together in this book, let's just rip off another Band-Aid of shame.

You may as well know that for years, I'd emasculated Michael. I'd make disparaging side comments at Michael's expense. I'd prop myself up as the more valued, more intelligent, more capable one - sometimes in public, sometimes just between us. It wasn't something I was particularly conscious of. My realization only came when he shot me a look of hurt or sometimes anger, and I'd feel ashamed and get angry at myself. I'd seen women emasculate their men so many times, and I judged them quickly for it. Yet I had a nasty habit of it too.

I beat myself up about it, but I could never seem to catch myself before a remark would escape my mouth. It felt instinctive, and I didn't know how to stop, so I shamed myself internally and flogged myself with judgment, lowering my fragile self-esteem further.

And it impacted our intimacy without a question.

So about nine months into my self-care journey, I heard Stefanos say the following, and it hit like a lightning bolt of truth:

"You won't need to emasculate him, if you can meet your own needs."

And I realized right then that when I took care of myself, I didn't take it out on those around me. I didn't lash out. I didn't blame them for my burdens and overwhelm. I wouldn't attack because I felt so vulnerable.

At some point I realized, like a kid who stopped sucking their thumb and didn't realize they were doing it, that I hadn't emasculated Michael in months! (I confirmed this was the case, of course, because I already divulged how dull my radar was for this behavior), but he agreed, and it blew my mind.

One of the incredible natural shifts that took place for me in taking two hours was how taking care of myself benefited the people around me most. I was happier. I was healthier. I was a priority. My needs mattered. For two hours a day, I was focused on how I was doing as a human being, and when I filled that cup, a lot of dysfunctional side effects of depletion stopped cold, and, of cours,e without the hurdle of emasculation present, deeper sexual and emotional connection was present in my relationship.

10 MONTHS TAKING TWO:
Kings and Foreplay

In the midst of these realizations, I was still having more sex than ever and actively seeking to explore more and experience new things, but the biggest breakthrough for me when it came to partner sex was mental rather than physical. I believe the largest sex organ we have available to us is our brain. The way to turn a woman on is through her mind first, before you touch her. Right, ladies? We know this.

One key learning came from listening to a podcast as I drove to my ocean view lookout. It was so good. I kept listening in my earpods as I hiked. I had tuned into another of Aubrey Marcus's episodes with he and his wife, Vylana Marcus, where they were talking about their sacred union. The thing that struck me was the vocabulary they used. They referred to each other as My King and My Queen.

At first, it sounded really weird to me, and I wasn't into it. But curiosity is one of my favorite traits, and I kept listening to how their story unfolded. I couldn't ignore the reverence they exuded for each other, and I felt like the terms King and Queen had a lot to do with reminding them of the level of presence and intention their connection deserved.

My relationship needed more reverence too. After nine years, it was too damned easy to take Michael and our relationship for granted. I thought, maybe it would be sexy to picture Michael as a king. Maybe tonight I'd go home and have sex with a fucking King. At first it felt so cheesy and almost sacrilegious, until I kept repeating the thought in my head, "not any King, my King." And, woah! That was a powerful difference. I highly recommend having sex with a King. One of your choosing. It was such a profound mental distinction that afterwards, I couldn't connect to him like I used to. When I pictured him as my King,

I not only desired him more, but how I touched him changed. It was reverence. It was respect.

For a King I could relax. I could let go of control. I could slip into being a receiver of love and allow him to give it. I had to be present. I had to be available, and I had to be open.

It was so powerful a mindset shift that I wanted to integrate it beyond our sex life. What if I held him in such high esteem and treated him with such reference outside our sex lives? It could function like foreplay. But I had an instant block. It would require a pretty massive shift from me specifically in our daily communication.

We work together. I was the CEO and more dominant and demanding. I thought about the times I'd cut him down with my words in public, undermined his reasoning, or acted like I had all the right answers. There were times I was abrasive or irritable with him, not letting him help me. I felt truly ashamed. Thankfully, what followed, that sense of shame, was a gentle, loving energy reminding me I'm a work in progress and that if I don't take the time to recognize harmful thought patterns, I won't be able to transform. This was what growth looked like.

I learned from Esther Perel that sexual attraction is all about polarization and that foreplay happens long before you reach the bedroom.

Foreplay isn't running around the first three bases.

It's kindness.

It's biting your tongue from criticizing.

It's stopping what you're doing to welcome your lover when they come through the front door.

It's in the tone of your voice.

It's in the winks or smiles you give.

I started to make a daily effort to be congruent and consistent with picturing Michael as my King and considering the larger landscape of foreplay. The energy and intention I set by myself transformed our connection. I think too often we think it takes two to shift. In this experience, I'd say it takes one, and the other will feel the vibrational change and react naturally to it.

11 MONTHS TAKING TWO:
Sex with a Soul

The day was perfection. I sat on top of my favorite hike overlooking Shell Beach. The entire ocean stretched out in front of me. Sunshine sparkled against the ripples in the peaceful body of water. I relaxed. I had everything I needed to soak up this time: sunscreen on my face, a time just be peaceful, and the luxury of no rush.

The meditation I'd listened to on the steep hike up to this point had shamanic drumming. I felt the beat resonate with every cell in my body. I wanted to keep the beat going but also wanted to meditate. Maybe there was a hybrid option online? I found one on YouTube that said Shamanic guided meditation. That sounded cool!

I closed my eyes and heard the deep, peaceful voice of a sage guiding me through an ancient forest, into a magical realm. Once the stage was set, the voice told me to watch and pay attention to anything that happens in my minds eye.

That's when I saw him.

I couldn't make out his facial features, but I could see he was perfect. The statuesque male physique that inspired some of the greatest pieces of art. He was naked, dancing around a fire with wild abandon.

I can't describe what happened in my body, but I was fatally attracted to this man. Still deep in meditation, I journeyed over towards him. He came right up to me, looked down, cupped my face and said, "You're the most beautiful," and then kissed me deeply. I proceeded to have the most electric sexual vision I've ever had. We were completely naked, truly free, and he was my guide, and I couldn't shake the feeling that my soul was at home with him.

The meditation finished, and I was so disappointed.

Then I felt guilty. *Did I just have sex during a meditation?* Weird. What would Michael think about that?

That vision stayed with me. One night I woke from a dream, and the same man was in my dream, and in my dream a voice spoke saying "Look deeper. What are you not seeing?" In my dream, my breath caught in my throat. *Michael!*

I woke up knowing the sexy man in my visions was Michael. His long wavy black hair, equal part warrior and lover, my soul mate. I had tears in my eyes. My intuition flooded in.

You experienced Michael's truest form of his soul. The man you felt so drawn to is the man you're married to, only he's free of conditioning. He was the purest form of his soul's expression. I knew it was true. I knew it was a sacred glimpse into the soul of my life partner, and it was a gift.

Later that day during my two hours, I sat by a river and thought about what that meant to me. I got a true glimpse into the soul of the man I loved. He was perfection in every way - so powerful, so safe, so confident, loving, and damn right majestic. I felt my heart explode with love for him. Even in his human form, I felt his soul inside of him. I felt so drawn to him at a soul level. I felt entrusted with the vision, so I could recognize all he is and the journey he is on in this life.

And then I thought, "How amazing would it be if he could have a vision of me in my most raw, pure form. What would I be like? How would I show up differently?"

I knew two things: my soul was not fully expressed in my human form yet and that this journey of undoing was bringing me closer to the fullest design of my soul.

CONCLUSION

When I started to take two hours a day, I thought I'd have good abs or take up some craft. Instead, I rehabbed my relationship to my sexuality, and while I know there is so much more to experience and explore, these shifts were profound and radically changed how I viewed my body, pleasure, and my husband.

My two-hour habit facilitated my sexual awakening at age 35, after nine years of marriage. If taking two hours a day could unearth something I was only mildly aware of, then what else could it do?

What I now know about exploring pleasure and sexuality is that it is not only the gateway to self-love but also to spiritual connection. Sexual expression has always held so much power. It's no wonder we've sought to control it and keep it contained. I find myself right now feeling like a rebel who is fighting an old system of oppression with every orgasm I give myself. Claiming my sacred right to experience pleasure on my terms and to turn myself on, to be so deeply connected to my creativity that an inspired thought may as well feel like universal foreplay.

And also to be okay that that intensity may subside as life presents new stressors or you navigate your partners' burnout or moods, and that's also okay. It's okay because you no longer need or rely on someone else to give you what your body needs, and you've stepped away from the performance of sex and embraced it as a genuine expression of in-the-moment desire and deep connection. Obligatory sex is not something either of us seek to participate in, and as soon as self-pleasure was allowed for each of us, a partner wasn't the only path to pleasure.

So what I'm playing with right now, since writing the above chapter about sex is:

Watching erotic movies with my husband and discovering which scenes were the most enticing for us and then reenacting them.

Introducing sex toys into our practice and really viewing sex as a practice in giving and receiving love in new ways.

Trying new ways to experience my body. Some days I buy an online course to teach me about having internal orgasms using jade eggs, because why the hell not? Other days I'm in a mastermind, and the assignment is to be alone and naked. To feel into any judgements or pain I still hold onto as I look at my naked figure. I am in a full place of exploration to deepen my relationship to pleasure and the love I have for my body.

chapter 10
STUCK MONEY

"I feel like we fell out of the lucky tree and hit every branch on the way down, ended up in a pool of cash and Sour Patch Kids."
- Ted Lasso

2 WEEKS TAKING TWO:
Visualizing Success in My CRV

In the beginning of my three-week trial at taking two hours, I discovered a YouTube channel called Rising Higher Meditation. I'm a sucker for a good Australian accent when it comes to relaxing meditations, and I found a 19-minute meditation that was perfect. It guided me into a visualization exercise.

It was basically a brainstorming session for everything a person might want to have in the ideal picture of their life - a vision board, if you will, and for someone who grew up perfecting the art of a good day dream, I was in my happy place. Well, not really. I was in my CRV with my pee jar next to me.

It was such a good experience that for a full week I kicked off my two hours with that same meditation. Pretty soon I could draw out the exact house design I wanted for my dream home. No joke! One night, I spent five minutes and sketched out a two-story, custom-built home complete with this crazy spa/dance studio/home office backyard house. Michael was impressed by the amount of detail. To this day, I know my future house inside and out.

But the craziest part, in my opinion, was how doing all these visualization meditations had reconnected me to how truly vibrant and exciting my inner world was.

The concept of having goals, knowing them, and revisiting them often wasn't new. Do you remember that 1979 Harvard study about goal setting as a predictor of success? The study found that 3% of the MBA graduates who had written down their goals actually made something like ten times more income than their peers. And this was only a decade after graduating. Now that's just writing down goals. I was sitting there visualizing more than my future house, in great detail, believing in that moment that it had to exist somewhere. It felt that real.

That visioning exercise reconnected me to my big audacious dreams, the kind you don't say in front of others for fear of being ridiculous or making them feel insignificant because their dreams were smaller. Suffice to say, when asked, I'd usually water down my dreams to match the comfort level of those around me.

The visioning exercises, however, encouraged me to dream big, beautiful dreams. It also reminded me that those dreams don't have to be diluted to be acceptable. They can be bold, whole, and audacious. I was always a child who day dreamed. These exercises brought me back into that childlike wonder that comes when you consider how many truly beautiful possibilities exist.

But you'll need a lot of money for that to come true. Money you don't have.

Oh yeah, money, the thing we had the least of in the midst of the pandemic. Our companies were bleeding thousands of dollars a month with no end in sight.

Doubt masked as realism poured water on all my dreams.

1 MONTH TAKING TWO:
Does God Hate Rich People?

I decided to go sit by a river, put my feet into the cold water and drink my hot herbal tea and just think. After four weeks of this two-hour habit, I'd decided to keep going and had learned how much I liked space to just think.

I had been listening to a lot of guided meditations that led me into what Abraham Hicks would call my vortex. (Essentially the vision board of the reality I wanted to be mine.) I'd see luxury, and my inner doubt would remind me of all the money having that would take and of all the hard work that it would mean. My inner dialogue would nag me about how if I'm already so burned out, how the hell did I think I could build the kind of wealth I would need to make these dreams come true.

And it was starting to annoy me.

I like dreaming and visioning, but I knew I had a scarcity mindset around money, believing there isn't enough to go around, thinking that if I have too much someone else won't have what they needed to care for their family … you know, that whole train of thought.

I put my feet in the cool stream and sipped on my ginger tea. Normally a devout bulletproof coffee connoisseur, I was surprised to like the vibe of the tea and the nature. I felt more hippie than normal, and it was good.

Then I started to let my mind wander. Sip after sip, thinking back to early memories about money. I knew exactly where to start. Witnessing a family friend's house burned down.

It was more than a memory from childhood, but it had for decades been for me the biggest cautionary lessons about money.

I remembered my hands were black. The soot was everywhere. My face was streaked like the little cinder girl, and I felt a heaviness all around me, stifling me. I was surrounded by chaos, grief and judgment. My 9-year-old self thought it had been hours, hours of searching. Our distraught family friend asked if I could find her wedding ring in the ashes where her bathroom had been before the fire. If you've ever smelled a burned house, you know. The heavy smell of char is all consuming. It's a smell of desolation that seeps into your skin and permeates your being.

I remember feeling devastated for her kids, who had just lost their house. I was sad for the parents who had worked so hard to build a beautiful life together. And then I remember overhearing, "This is what happens when you idolize money and make success too important."

At 9, I'd apparently born witness to what God does to people who want more, people who succeed at building wealth. And that idea clung on to me like the smell of soot for years. Maybe God didn't approve of wealthy people. Or worse, did God actually punish rich people? So if we wanted to get into God's good grace, were we meant to be poor?

That didn't feel right to me at all. Not then. Not now.

I sipped my tea. This memory was profound for me because it was the first time I remember being worried that when I made money, it could be taken away by a freak accident by an angry God.

Did I grow up thinking God was more of the champion of the lowly and friend to the meek?

I wondered if s/he was the lover of the least of us. So how did s/he feel about the wealthy?

Or maybe God just wanted to be the provider for the impoverished. Maybe that mattered so much to God that s/he became the instigator of tragedy to bring us low and slap us back into submission? Ew, that didn't feel good. It's hard to want to love a God like that, and I wanted to love God.

That was what I knew at age nine. But by my teens, I had absorbed a whole lot more that perpetuated this view that God disapproved of seeking wealth and success. Messages about money were dropped in every day conversation all the time.

I sat there journalling all the one liners I'd picked up over the years from friends, family, and teachers.

"He's sacrificing spending time with his kids for a paycheck."

"If only she had spent less time worrying about making money, she wouldn't be struggling to let her kids go to college."

"Well, they made their choice. Now she has to live with the consequences."

"You couldn't pay me enough to be away from my family and what really matters."

"They made money more important than the health of their relationship."

I had spent most of my life under the impression that having wealth came at a cost to things like family and happiness. I found myself in conflict early in life around money. While some part of me had believed the lesson that I probably should never aspire to any wealth or success. Yet, I knew deep in my heart that I would be wealthy. I knew not to share this awareness publicly as a young girl, but in my heart, no one could have convinced me that I wouldn't be rich one day. I knew it like a child knows their last name. I can't explain why. I just always, even from a young age, identified with wealthy people. So when "rich people" were openly criticized, I felt like *I* was being criticized. Even when my personal bank account was overdrawn and I owed the bank hundreds of dollars in overdraft fees, even then I knew it was a temporary reality that didn't match up yet with where I was heading.

But that conviction didn't protect me from worrying in the back of my mind that at some inopportune moment God could strike and bring me low because of it. The contradiction of feeling destined for financial success and scared it was all a ticking time bomb for an act of God to rip it away from me, plagued me for most of my life. It's honestly no wonder I have had a conflicted relationship with money and what it really represents—success.

I got up from the river, because of course I had to pee from all that tea, and made my way to the public restrooms this time. On my way there, I thought about that childhood fear of God taking it all away. I knew it was a deep fear of mine. I wanted to get rid of it but didn't know how.

TWO MONTHS TAKING TWO:
That Time I Got Depressed On a Flight to Mexico

A couple days after I'd sorted through the memory of the burned house on one of my two-hour times, I ventured down memory lane again. This time it happened while I was walking barefoot on the beach, letting the icy Pacific surf numb my feet. I wanted to revisit an executive exercise I'd done about money from 30,000 feet up in the air.

I had located my seat on the plane next to my business bestie and sighed. I was on my way to Cabo, Mexico for a four-day, exclusive retreat for 7- to-8-figure CEO leaders. No kids, no cooking, no cleaning, just showing up to strategize and learn with other badass leaders. It was exactly what I needed. But I still couldn't relax, at least not yet.

Like a classic procrastinator, I pulled out the book I was supposed to read before the retreat. I hadn't been able to check that off my list before boarding the plane. Seeing the book, my friend said, "Oh, I haven't even read a single chapter. Oops." I admired her because of the ease in which she was letting herself off the hook. Sadly, I'm not a catch and release kind of girl. I'm more of a hook, line, and sinker girl.

I had time on the flight, and I wanted to put it to good use, and one to-do item was not checked off. I was going for it. Could I get through a book about healing my relationship with money in two hours? I had to try.

I flew through Chapter 1 and made it to Chapter 2, which was all about unpacking your childhood beliefs and memories about money. *Sigh* Oh shit. Here we go. Therapy in a book. Someone should have warned me.

This wasn't a financial IQ book. This was a soulful deep dive on understanding all the bullshit beliefs I have about money that are blocking my success. Was I really ready to kick off my "no-kids vacation" like this? Too late. I'd already started.

I made my way through the questions. When was your first memory about money? What money beliefs did your parents, grandparents, extended family, or friends teach you?

In the end, you have a laundry list of every belief you have had about money.

It wasn't hard to come up with beliefs once I got going. I didn't filter the list. I just wrote and let the beliefs pour out of me.

Here are a few:

- Love of money is evil.
- Good people are taken care of through God's benevolent handouts
- Wealth will come one day, if you work hard enough.
- Money is unpredictable. It can be here one day and gone the next. Fortunes shift.
- Wealthy people figure out how to work smarter not harder.
- Trying to make money is a stress and burden.

- Money solves so many problems and is worth sacrificing for.
- Wealth comes at a high cost.
- Money is the product of hard work, smart timing, and shows success.
- Whenever I need money, it's always there.
- Money does not equal joy or a fulfilled life.
- I have anxiety around not having enough money.
- Hard work is toil and a curse God placed on us.
- Life is like a big game of Monopoly, and at the end of the day, you need money to win.

I stared at the list. It made no sense. Literally, it was a cesspool of contradictions. It was impossible to believe all of these at once.

I was slightly embarrassed with how unexamined the list was. I mean, I was in my early 30s marking three decades of believing contradictions?

A shitty realization.

The next assignment was to go through my list and identify what emotion I felt when I believed each of them. Great. On the great subject of money, the topic every CEO should master … here's how it made me feel:

- Shame
- Blame
- Fear
- Pride
- Sadness
- Resentment
- Helpless
- Satisfaction
- Hope
- Anger

The plane landed.

If money had been a person, we would have ended our relationship right then and there. Much like the conclusion I'd made about breaking up with my college boyfriend: for every good reason to stay together, there were two reasons to break up, and if you've ever been there, you know as well as I do that the yo-yo effect is more soul-sucking than the inevitable breakup.

I felt depleted, discouraged that I'd used my time to basically get depressed in mid-air. I went into my CEO leadership retreat feeling angry and conflicted about what the hell to believe about money.

Like the topic of sexuality, it didn't take long to piece together that not only did spiritual gurus talk openly about their orgasmic sex life, but they also seemed to talk openly about money. Not only talk about it, but teach about how to … what did they call it? Oh yeah, how to "call it into your life."

I kept walking along the beach, thinking of that experience and the list of contradictions. Had I made any progress since then? It had been years after all.

Nope. Without taking two hours, when would I have made time to just wander and wonder about things like wealth consciousness? I didn't know. So I was determined to spend some of my two hours thinking about wealth and success.

4 MONTHS TAKING TWO:
They Should Change the Song Title from "Money & Fame" to "Money & Pain"

It was raining. Probably one of the 10 days a year it rains in drought-ridden southern California. I was thrilled. Wearing my rain boots for the first time in 300 days and finally getting to use the rainbow umbrella

I'd treasured for a decade. I'd bought it in London as a broke teenager because I was so desperate to gain shelter from a torrential downpour that I actually bought the damn thing for £30, which at the time was like buying an umbrella for $55. It was a treasured relic. I obsessed about getting the "price per use" down to a reasonable 2 cents per use. Living in California certainly wasn't helping.

Why are you wasting time thinking about how much money you spent on this stupid umbrella? You're eating into your two hours!

But that's the thing, I started to realize four months in, there are no random thoughts. Our thoughts simply offer a new line of thinking to go down.

So I followed this one, and it led me to this idea: The subject of money is historically painful for all of us.

When I thought about money, it always seemed accompanied by pain. Like when I walked down the hallway at school wearing my favorite shirt for the second time that week, and within thirty minutes I was made fun of because I hadn't rotated through enough clothes for the popular girls to be appeased. I remember feeling hot and flushed. The truth was I didn't have thirty outfits to rotate through. I experienced shame and humiliation.

All because of a lack of money.

When I realized my friend was crying at lunch break because everyone had been making fun of him for smelling badly because his working mom couldn't make it to the laundromat that week, I felt my chest constrict in a deep pain. I felt guilty that I didn't have that issue, and I felt sadness for his misfortune, which wasn't his fault.

All because of a lack of money.

But on the other hand, when you land an internship in London and answer the question in Customs "Are you here for business or pleasure," with the truth, "I'm starting a sweet internship," only to realize you should have lied because you don't have a proper work visa and risk deportation. Which eventually is exactly what happened, but only after you were strip searched in a room where any sudden movements would result in a full lockdown, and you were sent in disgrace to the airport detention center, where you are rationed soggy egg sandwiches every four hours, then you get sent back to America with a red "deported" stamp in your otherwise colorful passport. Yes, this happened. I was sent back in a town where I had no job, had sublet my room for the summer, and because of all the phone calls I made from the airport detention center, had resulted in my bank balance being -$449. Damned Bank of American and it's $3.00 overdraft fees!

I was in financial debt because of a simple mistake.

And there are times when you lie to cover your lack of money. Like the time I said I was too tired rather than go out to dinner with my friends, too embarrassed to admit I'd been living off of the same Thai green curry base for weeks and had been trying to bring my price per meal down to under a couple dollars to make it to my next paycheck. And their pizza dinner promises to be $20, which would break my bank.

All because of a lack of money.

When you have to spark the solenoid of your white Aerostar van with a steak knife to get the ignition to work so you can start your car, and you do this every day for six months because you can't afford to fix the car all because the start-up you work for has been on the cusp of securing a series A round and hasn't paid you in months to make the company financials look more appealing. And you park around the corner from wherever you're going because the clothes you borrowed from a friend make you look like a million bucks but that car you rolled in would tear down the facade.

All because I didn't have money.

But then you realize you've still got a lot of privilege and realize, for the first time, that entire neighborhoods have been red-lined by financial institutions and assigned extortionate mortgage rates because of the "higher risk" of minority home buyers. You know that schools in those neighborhoods are funded based on the property values, which are far lower, meaning the access to education is bare minimum. And you also realize that you've benefited from this because you're white. Your neighborhood property rates are high, your kids' schools are fully funded, and your mortgage rates are incentivized.

All because money is a weapon used to continue to discriminate against minorities.

I'm still figuring this shit out in my 30s. I can't imagine what it's like for people who have a lifetime of painful experiences around money. These are just some of my money stories. And I know you could tell some too.

Suffice to say that if money were a person, we'd have a lot of repressed conflict. It also means that if money were a person, they probably wouldn't feel good being in my company, believing all this about them. The feeling is mutual.

The rain stopped, and I decided to head outside to enjoy that fresh smell of wet concrete.

FIVE MONTHS TAKING TWO:
When It Clicks It Just Clicks

Everything changed for me the day I realized money was simply energy. And that realization hit me between the eyes during one of my two-hour times when I was driving out to the ocean. I was listening to a podcast by my friend Christina Rice, who was talking about manifestation. Everything in life is a vibration, and the more you raise your vibration, the more you can connect to higher vibration things and people. And money, rather the abundance of money, is a high vibration, and the lack of money was a lower vibration, and vibrations can be altered, much like emotions. As I type this, I'm literally wearing an obnoxious yellow graphic tee that has a happy/sad face with the words "you decide," because I believe most of us can decide to be happy or sad each day. We have the power to choose it.

So why can't we see having the abundance of money or the lack of money as a matter of whether you're in a high or low vibration? We attract what we are. If we're in a low vibration, we attract low-vibration experiences, but if we're in a high vibration, we attract high vibration experiences. Woah.

My brain instantly started to connect past concepts I'd known and link them to this idea.

Like in Carol Dweck's book, *Mindset*

— Was having a growth versus a fixed mindset essentially a low versus high vibrational outlook?

Or in Jim Dethmer, Diana Chapman & Kaley Warner Klemp's book, *The 15 Commitments of Conscious Leadership*

— Is the concept of being above the line actually the same as being in a high vibration?

— And when we drop below the line, are we stooping into low-vibrational behavior?

How about The Enneagram?

— Is high vibe being the best version of your type and low vibe basically being that super creepy basket case at the dysfunctional level?

I could keep going.

My brain was running like it was on steroids, my entire body lit up in chills. Chills for me, at this point in my two-hour habit, meant it was spiritual confirmation that I'd hit truth. I had broken through the veil to the other side and everything was making sense.

Essentially, most frameworks around how to become successful could be boiled down to ... when you shift into a high vibration, good things are attracted to you, and when you shift into a low vibration, bad things are attracted to you.

Therefore, all your life experiences are being created by YOU. If there is a more uncomfortable thought, I'd love to hear it, particularly from the viewpoint of someone without my privilege. I started to ruminate in my highly sensitive, obsessive way. I put the car in park, headed up to my favorite perch, above what we locals call Pirates' Cove, and proceeded to deconstruct this. I went through everything I'd been told about becoming successful and how annoyed I was at every fucking millionaire who preached mindset.

I finally landed that they weren't talking about success. They weren't talking about making millions. They were talking about living a high vibration life, and from that place everything they sought was readily available. And therein lies the key.

7 MONTHS TAKING TWO:
Meeting the Empress

One day I took my two hours late in the evening and decided to play with my new Tarot deck and my pendulum, (something I could have never in a million years have thought I would do, much less admit to by way of a published book). My pendulum, by this point, gave incredibly clear answers to yes and no questions. Feeling playful, having the time and knowing Michael was fully absorbed in his favorite Formula One Netflix series, I did something new.

I asked my pendulum to show me which card in the card deck was closest to my soul's identity.

We yes'd and no'd our way through the deck and finally came down to one card.

I flipped it over, and bam, there was the Empress. I read the description excitedly. The Empress brings abundance and blessing to life. She is connected to material wealth and feminine creativity. My body lit up in chills. I smiled. It was a good card.

9 MONTHS TAKING TWO:
Magical Dancing On the Side of the Mountain

I had started to dance often during my two hours. In part, because it made me feel sexy and dancing had become part of my whole sexual expression, but I started to do it more because one day I found a song that just inspired dance. I mean the song "Footsteps in the Stars" by Deya Dova has probably been played hundreds of times on my Spotify. I didn't know how to listen to it and not dance, and the more I danced to it, the more I could tell there was a dance forming, a sequence of movements that felt inspired and magical. I don't know how else to describe it. It was always to that one particular song.

One day, I went out to this secret lookout spot away from the tourists, overlooking Shell Beach, and stood on the edge of this cliff with the sun on my face and my arms stretched out. I could easily imagine I was in the cosmos surrounded by my ancestors, angels and holy beings. I felt powerful and would play that song and just let movements flow out of me. As I danced, I visualized exactly what I was calling into my life, those visualizations, those specific images I had imprinted in my memory.

But this time it wasn't like brainstorming. This time I stood there like the Empress, creating exactly what I wanted to experience, and my dancing movements called it in, reaching for it and pulling it towards me with my body.

Every cell in my body knew I'd stumbled upon some kind of magic.

And the momentum was building.

10 MONTHS TAKING TWO:
Holy Shit This Works!

My two-hour habit was valuable for deep uninterrupted thinking, and it was also great for trying things consistently over time. I started out knowing a decent amount about mindset and nothing about manifestation, so every night, while doing dishes or every time I drove without the kids, I'd listen to podcasts or YouTube videos about it. My brain soaked this stuff up.

One day I listened to Christina Rice's podcast Christina the Channel, and she described how belief plays a huge role in manifesting, that and patience. She says that it's like going to a restaurant and looking at a menu and telling the waiter that you want spaghetti and meatballs. The waiter tells the chef and the chef starts to make it. But you flag down the waiter and change the order to lobster rolls. Then the waiter rushes back to the chef, who tosses out the spaghetti and starts to thaw the lobster meat. But then you send the waiter back twice more because you can't make up your mind. After an hour, you still haven't eaten, and now you're mad.

Well, no shit, Sherlock.

Your order was being made each time, but you kept redirecting the energy, and you're still hungry.

So what I took away from this was … Be clear. Be consistent. Be patient. Believe that it's on its way to you.

As I peeled back layers of protection and programming during my two hours, I found I possessed an incredible ability to believe in miracles. I credit my religious upbringing here because it taught me how to easily apply unwavering belief to concepts, the kind of belief that was innocent and pure. I knew it was its own kind of superpower.

Like Ted Lasso's sign in the locker room: BELIEVE, I felt like I had sent a rocket of belief up into the universe, and every time I visualized, or did my manifestation dance, I felt deep faith anchor me into some kind of frequency of miracles, and right around this time, I started to realize some major manifestations.

Now if we're going to talk about money and manifestation, I feel like it's important to be assured that the person you're listening to about manifestation isn't still living in their shoebox apartment, pinching pennies behind the scenes. I mean, that's where my faith starts to falter. So I'll share the most recent manifestations.

I manifested a career opportunity that literally got me unstuck in my career and pulled me into the opportunity to double our family's income. I manifested a business that was on a six -figure run rate by month two, closing my ideal clients.

I manifested getting my daughter off of a waitlist for a preschool in a town where preschool waitlists build to hundreds of kids.

I manifested a five-figure check out of thin air for our business.

I manifested a six-figure personal check out of nowhere.

I manifested three different people telling my husband and I that they'd be happy to provide any financing we'd need with zero interest.

And then I manifested seven figures in funding for my other business. It was wired to us on 2.22.22. A very magical day to me because it was also the day my red Tesla Model Y with white interior was delivered to me, which just added to the magic.

And one of my favorites is manifesting a hot seat coaching with Jessica Zweig, Chicago's top personal branding guru. I knew she'd pick a participant to coach, and as soon as I heard she'd do that, I thought, "It'll be me." Again, with that complete childlike belief. I just knew. The email telling me I'd been chosen didn't even come as a surprise, more of a validation.

I decided I didn't want to self-publish this book and manifested meeting a publisher. Two weeks later I signed an agreement with a publisher.

Like seriously, is this real life?

And what's even more wild is that I know in my soul that I am only just beginning, and I'm going to be kicking myself when this book finally publishes that I didn't push out the publishing date so that I could include even more manifestations.

CLOSING

Since doing my visualization or manifesting dance for about 20 minutes during most of my two-hour blocks, I've seen massive wealth shifts, and instead of coming with hard work, it was coming with ease.

And when you read this, I don't want you to ask, "Why did this all happen for her?" I want you to challenge yourself to ask, "Why can't this be me?" Because that's what I did the first time I heard my mentors discuss what miracles they'd witnessed.

Of course, Pleasing Prudence said, "*Oh, it's not nice to talk about money. Shame on you.*" And Bitchy Brittany added, "*Who the hell do you think you are, God?*"

And instead I dared to think, "If they can, then so can I." And that's why the magic of making space for myself for two hours a day helped me reverse my confusion around money and step into a manifestation practice that has yielded incredible results in a short time. I now firmly believe that when we raise our vibration, we begin to attract higher vibrational realities And my two-hour habit gives me the chance every damned day to recalibrate my vibration to a higher level, the level that attracts money and abundance.

What I now know about money is that it is energy and one worth getting to know. There continues to be a lot of resistance around earning and deserving money as a result of hard work. This is actually a topic Michael and I still don't see eye to eye on. I have been increasingly sensitive to comments that assume you have to earn money and that it's not an energetic expression of divine alignment. As I disentangle from my people pleasing tendencies and allow myself to be in my own truth, understanding how the frequency of money works is still very much a work in progress.

For example, one day during my two hours I was walking on the beach and my inner voice said, *'Turn around and watch that woman throwing a ball to her dog."* Perplexed, I watched a woman fit a tennis ball into her chucker and then launch it into the whitewash of the ocean. What caught my eye was the dog. Before she even raised the chucker overhead, the dog was running full speed into the water, turning quickly to be ready to receive it. Instantly, I knew the deeper lesson. I was the dog and the Universe or God was the woman throwing the ball. I needed to trust so emphatically that the desires of my heart and those better than I could imagine were going to be thrown my way. I just had to be in position to receive them. It was such a powerful visual for me. It felt playful. It felt repetitive. It also felt like you could miss a ball once in a while and still come back to play again.

So what I'm playing with right now when it comes to the topic of money is:

Staying playful with money. Like the dog running in full faith into the surf, waiting to catch the ball, I plan to keep running back into that whitewash in anticipation of gifts and money I haven't hustled for.

Becoming friends with the personification of money. I've determined that the embodiment of money is a well-dressed, refined, and hilarious woman named Iris. Don't ask. It's the first name that popped into my head during my visualization. I imagine talking to her, laughing with her, welcoming her into my friendship and being welcomed into hers. I visualize her wanting to be in my energy and enjoying my company, and I sense it's changing my relationship with money, which historically would have been a miserly, grumpy old man happy to report how little I'd earned. No, Iris was better.

Opening my arms, literally, and letting the sunlight stream into my outstretched arms. Seriously, picture me on the side of a sunny hillside, imagining a sparkly golden light funneling blessings into my heart and life. I visualize all my wildest dreams funneling right into my reality.

I get ready in the mornings listening to YouTube compilation videos about celebrities and famous people talking about law of attraction and manifestations. It's the most motivational content I've found. It reminds me of the power of setting an intention and asking for your desires.

chapter 11
UNTETHERED SOUL

"We're gonna try it on and see if it fits. It might not. Then again, it might be a very flattering silhouette. I might wear it right out of the store. Makes me feel good, start to strut. Oooh, I like this. I like the way this makes me feel."
- Ted Lasso

2 WEEKS TAKING TWO:
Intuition Bootcamp

I sat there in my car. It was too cold to go on a hike. Which as a Californian from the Central Coast means it was 55 degrees Fahrenheit. And today I didn't mind because I was hell bent on unlocking my intuition. I had started to embrace the idea that it was a muscle that needed to be strengthened to be reliable. So I was working on understanding how my intuition worked. I had a little checklist of all the ways people experienced their intuition: dreams, visions, seeing angel numbers, getting thoughts that weren't theirs but they knew were true, even getting full body chills when something was right.

> Right out the gate, I tried to gamify my two hours into a full-blown intuition development bootcamp. I was both sergeant of my results and tortured athlete. I was militant about trying to open that elusive third eye. That is a phrase that before Sedona would have meant nothing to me. But since Sedona, intuition felt like the seat of all my mysterious powers. Are we even surprised that the "overachiever" who face planted in my own kitchen hit the ground running trying to turn soul restoration into an opportunity to achieve results? It's so damned ironic. But performance is my default mode, and I hadn't undone that part of me. I didn't catch how counter-productive this was for a while. I was too obsessed with figuring out this thing called intuition.

What became clear to me, the more I learned about how intuition can show up through our senses, I started to remember stories of how my intuition showed up my whole life. As a child, I could lucid dream and banish demons from my dreams. I could sense if someone was unsafe or the energy was off in a room in a split second. I would sometimes be talking to someone and instantly know very personal things about them, things like whether they'd been abused as a child. Wild information that, to be fair, I couldn't always validate but still had a deep knowing that it was true. As a consultant, I'd get these premonitions or inspired ideas that as soon as they came out of my mouth would be validated in one way or another, securing the admiration in the room. I marveled at the random information that would come into my brain.

What I realized in Sedona was that it was like a muscle and had to be strengthened to be called upon to predict outcomes with accuracy. I was determined to harness my intuitive powers, but laughably, I knew so little about intuition much less how to develop it, so I obsessed for weeks about finding the perfect intuition development meditations. The results didn't happen overnight, and I felt annoyed.

Finally, I made peace with something. The goal of the two hours wasn't to become an intuitive powerhouse. It was to bring my soul some peace. Feeling frustrated over my lack of "alone time results" was hurting the overall mission.

So I gave up on trying so damned hard, remembering that I was supposed to figure out how to be a human being and stop making everything about doing or achieving something.

I took a breath and let myself off the hook, and ironically, doing so was ultimately what catapulted me into a true spiritual awakening.

1 MONTH TAKING TWO:
Are You Even Real?

I climbed up on a large boulder on top of the tallest peak in San Luis Obispo. I breathed in the fresh air and found a less pointy part of the rock to sit on. I had religion on my mind, and I just wanted to look out over an epic view and just think.

Before taking two hours a day, I was on the fence about being Christian. I grew up knowing a lot about God, even studying it at Capernwray Bible school in England for a year before going to college. I could quote the Bible and argue Apologetics with almost anyone, but it lost its luster, and I fell out of love with the tradition of religion. I was so jaded by the rules and endless striving to be good enough that I couldn't even look at the Bible without wanting to throw up.

My relationship with God was the confusing part. I didn't know what to do about God. I wanted to love God and know God, but I couldn't find a way to stomach the ways loving God were being served up by religious groups.

Long before I'd gone to Sedona to confront my soul's unrest, I remember going to bed one night and saying in my head, "God, are you even real? I don't know if I believe that anymore."

I woke up to what I could only describe as a deep voice that said, *"You know I'm real."* I was stunned and thrilled all at once that this massive voice had responded to me. From then on, I clung to the belief that God existed, but I didn't know how to make my way to God. Deep down, I knew it had to be outside of religion. Religion was just too triggering for me.

You see, as much as my adult self was angry and blaming religion for how unhappy I turned out to be, the child inside of me wanted God to be real, wanted to know and be loved by God. That part of me, the curious truth-seeker, was alive and well. That question asker, that thinker that preferred the unstructured discovery of a great mystery, I wanted to go on this quest. I just needed to get out of my own way and be open to it looking differently than I was raised to believe it should be.

That very day I gave myself permission to stop pretending to be a Christian. I told God, "Okay, if you're real, help me to find you."

For the last five years, I had stopped going to church regularly, stopped reading my Bible, and stopped defending the faith. I stopped asking to get healed, and I went in the direction of self-healing. I focused on personal development, chipping away at things like inner child healing, shadow work, mindset rewiring etc., and of course, I doubled down on work and hitting my professional goals. Then life heated up again when I became a mom and motherhood became an all-consuming path to growth.

That being said, as soon as I became a mom, I felt so much pressure to "figure out spirituality" because I worried that when my daughter turned five and wanted answers, I wouldn't have good ones. But no answers came, and I wasn't about to settle for basic answers to deep questions, so I remained in limbo spiritually.

And then I got pregnant with Jackson, and from that minute on, something shifted inside me. My discontent with my life professionally and spiritually couldn't be shoved conveniently into the crevices of my soul. There's no other way to explain it. I felt a soul nudge daily that I wasn't doing what I was designed to do. I was in a crisis of purpose, and when you're in that place, when you still believe in a soul designer of some kind, your soul gives you no rest.

3 MONTHS TAKING TWO:
What Napa Wine Region Taught Me About God

Phew! I'd just hiked up, at record speed, Islay Hill and had broken a sweat. I stood up at the top, hands on my hips, my chest heaving trying to catch up. I shielded my eyes and looked over my favorite valley in San Luis Obispo, Edna Valley. It is a celebrated wine region in our wine county. Garnering national recognition and being a less pretentious version of Napa Valley, you really couldn't attend a single social event without local wineries pouring. I stood up there marveling at the beautiful view and thinking about the wine industry.

Yep, that's what happens when you're a business consultant or entrepreneur. You start to think about the pros and cons of the business models in the most random moments.

I smiled to myself, remembering my rather hilarious initiation into the wine tasting scene.

If you ever get invited by your friends to join them for a classy, estate wine tasting … and if that wine tasting happens to be in Napa,

California … the answer is always yes. Just yes. Especially when you and your husband collectively make $50K per year where the poverty line in California is $57k for double income families, and thus rarely afford more than the two buck chuck Charles Shaw wine from Trader Joe's.

Well, we got that invite long before kids, and we said that yes. Then we scoured our house to figure out what the hell to wear for such an occasion and worried about whether we'd be sophisticated enough guests when we couldn't honestly tell the difference between a $2 bottle of wine and a $100 bottle of wine. One of my college friends and her husband were members at an incredible winery in Napa, which included an exclusive four-person estate tasting. We were flattered to be their pick of friends to bring. I remember driving up together seeing the French Chateau estate's exterior and feeling a mixture of excitement and nervousness. I have always loved the finer things in life, but at that time in my life had rarely experienced them.

I will never forget the wine tasting. We were greeted by someone wearing a butler's uniform, you know, the black suit with the tails? Yep. He asked us to take a seat in a private study. We walked into a room with dark mahogany walls, hunter green wallpaper, and books neatly stacked on the book shelves. There was a table with two brown leather chairs by a window that overlooked the grounds, but the setting was not nearly as fancy as what was to follow. We were escorted up a curved stone staircase and into a room with a balcony overlooking the vineyard. A table had been prepared for us, set pristinely with three different forks, several shapes of glassware, and the table had an exquisite display of fresh flowers.

It was fancy. I was not. I tried, but I was still wearing flip flops underneath a maxi beach dress and a winter brown coat over the top because, of course, I was cold. Part of me felt self-conscious, but in our own private room, who cared? We could have been in sweats and no one would have seen. Remember, this was all well before TikTok and Vasco girls who made baggy, unkempt style a thing. We were seated and then handed a small, formal tasting list of six exclusive wines we'd sample that afternoon. In truth, I couldn't have pronounced most of the wine names on that list. I felt like I was in France, and I couldn't pronounce anything, and rather than try and be made fun of, I'd awkwardly smile and just point to something on the menu and pray to God it wasn't anchovies.

Of course, the intimidating part of the tasting menu were the notes written by the sommelier. You know, the wine-snob-turned-guru, who developed their senses of taste and smell into such refinement that no establishment could possibly be fancy without retaining the services of a sommelier who knew how to curate their exclusive wine list. I remember reading the sommelier's notes for each wine, detailing the specific notes we should detect with each sip. Things like lavender, apricot, and even tobacco. I watched our server smell the wine, swirl the wine to watch the "legs" form on the glass. What the fuck? Wine has legs? I mean, I had been a server for years in a 4-star restaurant, and I knew the lingo, but hell if I actually knew what to look for or why it mattered. But I wish I'd listened more to all our staff wine training because I was swirling away and pretending to see legs. Then the server would take a small taste of the wine, swish it in their mouth, let it sit there probably until it was a lukewarm temperature, and only then would he swallow. I didn't know or understand why, but I followed. It's what you do in those settings.

And that was just the beginning of the day. We went to three more wineries that day, and with each change in location, our wine snobs' personas seemed to recede like a tide, giving way to our less sophisticated identities. We all wanted to be able to get the full Napa wine experience, so we followed their lead and tried to taste the exact notes we were supposed to. We turned wine tasting into a game, to distract us from how little Michael and I really knew. Our friends loved board games, so they went for it. We decided: let's not read any of the sommelier's notes and see if we can detect the correct flavor palette. Game on. We would follow the wine tasting protocol step-by-step for each wine and write down the key notes we deciphered and then compare with one another and ultimately use the sommelier's description as the answer key.

If I'd write down something floral, like lavender, Michael was sure to get something fruity, like cherry, and then that damned sommelier would say, "A slight note of graphite detected, followed by a shocking burst of citrus."

"No way," we'd exclaim. "How could we be so far off?" It was insane to us. So we persisted with both the wine drinking and the game to crack the flavor code of each wine. Our batting average tanked. The game was never intended to be hilarious. It started out in earnest. We wanted to get it right. All of us like winning. But the truth was apparent to every Silicon Valley executive witnessing our competition that was rapidly descending into hysterical and irreverent laughter, branding us novice wine drinkers to the dismay of all.

We took it upon ourselves to rewrite every single wine description with the most off-the-wall, ludicrous nouns we could think of. Our favorite was, "complex notes of shoe string leather with a symphony of lilac followed by an earthy plum truffle finish." Damn! Nailed that one. But no one else saw the humor.

By the fourth winery, we didn't even care. We were so focused on walking straight because when you earn as little as we did, and can't even afford $2 wine bottle. You aren't going to spit out the contents poured from a $100 bottle. You're going to swallow it and feel like you got the best deal of your life. Well, that strategy came with a price tag of not being able to walk straight without total focus. This led us into a mentally bolder space than we would have otherwise allowed. We became tipsy and miffed, which of course turned into boisterous, outright defiance of the oppressive wine tasting world. We almost became righteous about how wrong we were. How was it possible that we could all taste the same wine and come away with completely different experiences? We finally asked one of the girls pouring wine, and her answer was so simple.

"Oh, everyone's genetics determine what their taste receptors pick up on. We each have variations in the taste receptor genes which cause us to pick up on different flavors."

What? Then why write a description at all, as if we have to pick up on the exact same things to appreciate and understand wine? We gave up the game at that point, recognizing its futility. On the drive back home, I recall feeling validated that I wasn't wrong about all the flavors I'd tasted. I was just experiencing wine in my own way. I didn't need to feel the pressure to pick up a glass of wine and experience it like the person next to me. Wine wasn't just for snobs. Wine was for everyone. Wine was designed to be experienced by everyone and appreciated for how it shows up differently for all palettes.

I came out of remembering that funny story and stood up overlooking Edna Valley, just thinking there was no rush. I still had a good hour left of my two hours, so I stayed up there, looking at the perfectly symmetrical rows of vines giving structure to the gentle rolling hills. I thought back on that experience and started to play with the analogy of wine drinking being a lot like experiencing God. Everyone experiences God uniquely, which is what makes the experience so powerful and beautiful, but when you're in environments like church, or in this analogy, wine clubs, you can feel like you have to do it their way, taste what they say you taste, swirl and spit and swallow only as the wine snobs do. Which may feel refined and enlightening as an insider, but it can make it not only intimidating to outsiders but can make you talk and act superior to people like beer drinkers.

If wine clubs are churches in this analogy, what if wine members were church goers and sommeliers were pastors? I considered the parallels. It could work. A pastor typically went to school to study the Bible and bring curated truth to you as a spoken art-form, but could, perhaps, be considered to have superior knowledge that it runs the risk of robbing you of trusting your own personal exploration of God. It's like giving up your power and giving it away to someone else because you don't trust yourself to find God on your own. That seemed ass backwards to me. I wanted the ability to be more than a truth seeker, but also a truth finder.

As someone who lives in wine country and is friends with winery owners, I heard, "The biggest threat to the wine industry isn't the price of wine. It's the wine snobs. They intimidate new potential wine drinkers." That sentiment holds up in this metaphor because when it comes to religion, people don't often quote Jesus when taking up their offense with his followers. The wine isn't where the fault is found. It's found in the patrons: those chosen and righteous devotees out there representing their beliefs, judgments, and rejections as part of living out their faith. The harm that has been done by men and women in the name of God is the biggest barrier to religion, in my experience. There is a risk in this model that alienates people who don't want to follow the specific directions and experience like the rest of the wine club does. The barrier to entry for wine drinkers is higher, not only the price tag of the experience, but it requires time.

The wine was always meant to be experienced, tasted, and shared in celebration, and what if it was the same with experiencing God. What if the experience of the Creator, the Source of all, was designed to be individually discovered and there was no wrong way to develop a relationship with it?

Woah! My body lit up in chills instantly, my intuitive proof that I'd hit on something profoundly true. That felt like such a freeing and expansive thought. It certainly had merit. I thought it through on the way back to the car.

4 MONTHS TAKING TWO:
They Call it an Awakening

I was happily perched up at the top of a cliff overlooking an incredible panoramic view of the Pacific Ocean and three cute beach towns. What a life! My heart swelled. This was now my new reality. Mid week, here I was acting like I was on vacation. Yep, that is exactly what my two hours gave me, daily slices of being on vacation. It was like hitting a giant pause button on a life that was chock-full of responsibilities and expectations.

How did I even get here? This was seriously the best thing ever.

I felt so far removed from the restless soul that catapulted me into this awakening, but I had to give credit to Allyson Byrd's Soul Session group coaching program. It called to me. I resonated with her, and her teachings were the first to liberate me into discovering God in a new, expanded way. She talked about God as a she, which felt satisfyingly rebellious and freeing. She referred to Black Jesus, and this made me wonder why the hell blond-haired, blue-eyed Caucasian Jesus was the image I'd always had in my mind. WTF?

Then I thought about pronouns and the cultural space being made for people to identify themselves more freely. I found it peaceful to think of God not as a he or she, but truly as they. The original they, from a pronoun standpoint. A gender free, universal being.

This all brought me so much joy because it was testing me to rethink it all and be open to possibilities. It felt fresh. It felt exciting, and for the first time I saw a mentor who had a life I wanted, who prayed to Jesus still and yet had a much more expansive view of her spirit and purpose, and I wanted to learn what she knew. Which, as you know, sent me to Sedona on my soul adventure and taking my two hours a day.

Of all the topics I've shared with you in this book, exploring spirituality and who God is was one of the most impactful results of my two hours a day. Before Sedona, I thought I was fine being spiritually sober, but it became so clear to me after that I was deeply wounded and had so consistently self-betrayed to please religious authorities, that I didn't really know what I believed or wanted from God, and of course, once I realized how damned intuitive I had been my whole life, as a personal development junkie, I couldn't bear to *not* explore that potential. I started actively learning and exploring what my intuition had been trying to tell me.

I continued to confront my questions around what I believed about my spirit, the creator, the quiet voice in the back of my head that had been trying to partner with me through life. Even though I was still relatively stuck in spiritual indecision, I was actively considering my spirit daily and listening to my soul, that still voice that just needed some silence and curiosity to give it permission to speak.

I'd meditate on my soul and its path.

I'd hike and ask God to meet me and show me how to find a way to connect in a fresh way that could bring me back into a relationship.

I'd sit and stare out into the sky and think about if I really believed in heaven and spirits or spirit guides.

I just felt so deeply grateful for this journey. The freedom to sort through decades of experiences, sound bites, and random Bible versus that seemed to float into my consciousness just when I needed something to consider.

6 MONTHS TAKING TWO:
Did I Just Talk to Jesus?

Have you ever sat down somewhere and recalled a conversation in that same place that took place years before? I love when that happens.

One night, I took my two hours after the kids went to bed, and although it wasn't as cool as hiking in the sunshine of the morning, it was what I had to work with that night. I sat down at my kitchen table and suddenly remembered a conversation I had with my cousin and his wife a couple years earlier, at this exact table.

Somehow we'd gotten on the topic of religion and where I stood with God. I was open and shared how much I was in limbo. We related on some of the classic religious hang ups many share. I remember blurting out, "I feel like I'm going to have to find God outside of religion. I need a fresh experience of God to reconnect." My cousin nodded and said, "Well, if you find a way to experience God outside of church, let me know. I'd sign up."

The irony of that memory was incredible, given the journey taking two hours sent me on. I smiled, as I opened up my blank journal page.

I reflected for a minute on what I'd learned since that conversation at this kitchen table. I'd embraced that spirituality can coexist with religion, for the most part. Spiritual people don't have a problem with religious people who act in love. Spiritual people believe any path that leads you into a connection with God, and living a life infused with eternal love is not wrong. Religious people, however, have a problem with spirituality because it's broader and more expansive than what they've known to be true. This threatens the boxes they've built to feel secure in their systems. Yet, when I'd say I'm connected to God, they challenged me and said, "I don't know what God you pray to but it's not my God."

Spiritual people don't believe in just one holy text. They don't follow one path or one way of experiencing divinity. This makes them difficult for religious people to control, follow, and trust.

But does that make it wrong?

When you go back to the genesis of religion, it looks a lot more like spirituality looks today, a bunch of people trying to find and connect to God, people looking for wisdom, guidance, miracles, and leaders who are vessels for God's word to come through. This is how Jesus was discovered to begin with. He spoke, it resonated as truth, and people followed him and brought their friends. Organic growth.

I remember going on a hike and trying to make sense of how Jesus could be the way, the truth, and the life AND there could still be space for other belief systems? I mean, that is the cornerstone of Christianity, and in that space and with over an hour to contemplate this, I thought something I hadn't before.

What if Jesus was exactly who he said he was, the way to God? What if he was a truly powerful, spirit-filled example of what is possible for us all? What if Jesus, one of the most influential people in history, modeled for us how to actually live as both fully human and fully God?

Right then, the verse John 14:12 floated back into my awareness: "Truly, truly, I say to you, whoever believes in me will also do the works that I do; and greater works than these will he do…"

What if Jesus showed us what was possible as humans?

I stared at the blank pages of my journal and decided to try something new. I knew how to connect my spirit to God, so I did. Then I asked if Jesus was there and if I could speak with him. I felt chills and a warm, loving energy around me, and I knew Jesus was with me.

So I asked a simple question: "Where did Christianity go wrong?"

I started to write the words that came to me. *"They took truth intended for that day and time and turned it into dogma."*

Woah. Did I just talk to Jesus? I mean, I grew up praying at God but never like that. I thought a lot about the concept of taking truths and turning it into a system. The truth wanted to flow. The structure of religion wanted to capture truth and hold it safe.

7 MONTHS TAKING TWO:
Does Truth Evolve Like Nature?

I went on another hike just to observe nature, and after being out there for about an hour, a thought floated into my awareness: Everything that has been created must expand; to grow, seed and give way to more life.

Which means truth has to keep growing and seeing more truth or it's dead. For it to live, it has to keep evolving, and that's not what religion has done. Somewhere down the line a group of men got together and decided which texts were, in fact, holy and which ones weren't. This is how the sixty-six texts, which are now known as the Bible, were created, in Latin of course, so no one could read it but the clergy, but before it disbanded, this group also added some final thoughts to the book of Revelations that basically curses anyone who takes away or adds to the Bible.

Then I thought, has there ever, in the history of humanity, been a school of thought that consciously decided to stop evolving? To stop exploring? To stop iterating?

I couldn't think of any. I mean, what if the medical industry just decided, "Yep, we're good with the leeches and bleeding people out to get rid of infection. That's a wrap! Let's pause it all. And then let's shame and throw out anyone trying to further what we know." How insane is that? Yet, the Bible hasn't been added to since it was canonized (aka. turned into what we know as the Bible). It hasn't been expanded seriously in centuries. Hmmm. That was definitely food for thought for an entire hike or two.

I landed on considering that just because humans decided the Bible was complete, doesn't mean God did. Did God really just stop sending messages to humans that other humans could benefit from learning? Did God stop working miracles through humans? Or did the early church just want the safety and security of having a document be complete so they could turn it into a system and process and not have to constantly be evaluating what is somewhat true or mostly true and always be evolving the religious consciousness? I mean, if I was trying to lead and control a group of people, I could see how it would be more convenient to not have to pivot my message or evolve the model constantly.

Is that where religion went wrong? I believe so. To me the biggest casualty to religion is the lack of curiosity and expansion. It just stopped growing. It stopped evolving. It stopped seeking further enlightenment. It settled for only furthering intellectual interpretations, not new material.

Certainly not teaching people to develop their God given capabilities to intuit spirit messages in real time for their modern life. The very thing that was giving my soul flight.

8 MONTHS TAKING TWO: The Power of Animals on the Hiking Trails

I started to think a lot about Jesus saying we could do what he did and more. What did Jesus do? He spoke directly to God and God spoke through him. He performed miracles and could heal people by touching them. He could face down his adversaries and still feel love and compassion for them. He could create a reality if he wanted. What if we all could do that?

And as heretical as that idea may sound, it landed as truth in my heart.

So I started to dedicate some of my two hours to trying to connect to God and listen with my soul. I started to ask for signs. I tapped back into the childlike curiosity and even the skills to blindly believe what I couldn't see, and the benefit of taking so much time every single day to do something is that it builds quickly. I started seeing huge shifts.

After hours of meditating, I knew how to discern what were my own thoughts and what were not. I discovered just how many inspiring and genius ideas popped into my head that were not my own. The healers in Sedona would call that my clairaudience or clear hearing. Maybe God was giving me inspired ideas, wisdom to share that wasn't mine at all but was intended for those listening to me. That was a pretty cool thought.

I started to wonder if God could show me signs. I knew God could, but I wasn't sure how, so I just asked for some signs, and I started to notice how many birds there always were around me. So I Googled the spiritual symbolism of specific birds I could pick out, and the messages were profound.

It started with mockingbirds flying in front of my car, singing in every tree on my walk, their feathers dropping in front of me. I was offended by the first definition I found, "imitator, lacking authenticity and originality," but it was true. My whole life I felt like I was singing someone else's song. Was I singing everyone else's song still and hadn't found my authentic one yet? I made peace with the fact that that was okay because I didn't know what my song was - not in my career, not in my spirituality, but I trusted both would come to me.

Then I started to see more animals with more messages.

One day I was feeling anxious about money and navigating the pandemic. Would we make it? As I walked and worried, I couldn't help but notice all the rabbits darting about the fields. I quickly Googled "spiritual meaning of rabbits" and got "Good luck in love, family, and finances." It felt like a promise. Another time I was tired and feeling guilty for taking my two hours, and as I was hiking up a mountain, I started to notice how many lizards there were on the trail. There must have seen 100 lizards on the half mile trail. Weird? Or on purpose? I Googled it. The spiritual meaning of lizards was "regeneration and renewal". There I was taking two hours to regenerate my spirit. It was an encouragement.

9 MONTHS TAKING TWO:
Weird Ass Birds and Dodging Flying Ducks

Another day I specifically asked to see a new animal, one I hadn't yet seen. I started my hiking and wishing. About ten minutes in, a large funny looking bird crossed right in front of me. I had never seen it before. I had no idea what it was. I remember thinking, "What is that?" And the word popped into my mind, "*roadrunner.*" I pulled out my phone and checked. Sure enough, it was. The spiritual message was "Find the humor in situations, not taking life too seriously." I laughed out loud. I needed that.

One day, during my two hours, I remember being in conflict about whether to accept a job going back to business consulting. I had been running our family's fitness business but had felt that soul tug that I needed to do something different. But what? I asked for a sign. I stood by a creek on one of my hikes. I was just staring at the water. Then I ducked. A large duck flew right by my head. I was annoyed and doubted if it was a sign. So I asked God, if it's a sign, please send it back. Twice more during my meditation I saw that duck fly past me. The spiritual meaning of the duck that jumped out at me was "act now, recognize the opportunity in front of you and move swiftly." It felt like a powerful sign.

I then shifted to numbers and asked to see synchronistic numbers. I started to see 2:22 and 11:11 everywhere. I swear, four to six times per day I'd look down at my cell phone or computer and see repeating numbers that also carried relevant messages that spoke into my life.

This is when I really fell back in love with nature. Everywhere I looked, birds, animals, plants and just nature itself showed me messages and lessons. It has become a refuge for my soul. It speaks into my life daily, and most of what I do now is just spend time in nature thinking about whatever is on my mind, asking for signs and direction and just paying attention.

10 MONTHS TAKING TWO:
That Time My Life Coach Called Me a Bigot

Right around this time I'd concluded that I didn't need or value religion when it came to cultivating my spirit. It just wasn't for me, or rather it felt better to sit over in my spiritual camp, feeling more enlightened. Can you feel the tinge of arrogance with that? Well, I'm a believer in always having mentors in life who call you on your bullshit before it gets engrained, and my life coach (remember the German Buddha coach from Sedona? Yep, I hired her as my life coach) picked up on it quickly in one coaching session. She called me out on it and said something to the effect of:

"If you think about religious people as THEM and separate them from YOU, you're basically a bigot. How can you be mad at religious people for acting superior when you're doing the same thing from a different viewpoint? Creating out groups is one of the biggest causes of pain in humanity. Don't fall for it. Your greatest work in this life is to speak in love and with compassion."

Her words were profound, and my body lit up in chills, giving weight to how important this message was for me to embrace.

"You need to learn how to describe your connection to God in a way that doesn't alienate people with jargon that puts you in a separate camp than them."

I thought a lot about that feedback on one of my hikes. Had I just done the same thing I felt religious people do to me? But I was returning the favor as an "enlightened spiritually woke soul?" Yuck! I didn't want that at all.

I realized I needed to be more open minded.

The Universe served up an opportunity a couple weeks later when my parents came into town, and we danced around the awkward moment of them wanting to pray over me before they departed and my wanting to be respected for having different beliefs. Over the years, we came to a respectful understanding of our boundaries, but that night my Mom asked if she could pray for me. Normally I would have said, "No thank you, but thanks for the offer," but I wanted to be more open-minded and expand my view on how God connects to people.

I surprised everyone by saying, "Yes!" Michael's eyebrows went up, and he cracked a half smile as he bowed his head.

My mom prayed a heartfelt prayer, and something I never would have expected happened. As she prayed, all of our eyes were closed, and I felt the unmistakable beam of white light flood over me. I had no words. I knew this light intimately. This pure, bright, glittery light which had only prior come to me when I meditated. I believed this had shown me how superior my newly discovered path to God was, but here I was feeling the depth of my Mom's connection to God and witnessing how real it was for her and how similar her connection to God was to mine.

My view expanded right there and then, and I felt this peace in my heart that, even if I didn't resonate with religious groups AND even if I find some of the teachings to be harmful, I cannot discredit that for some religion offers the closeness to God that I found. God can be found. That divine white light that illuminates hearts isn't reserved for just one type of believer.

12 MONTHS TAKING TWO:
When a Philosophizing Mind Floats in Magnesium

I lay there in a float tank with nothing but my thoughts. Have you ever floated on the surface of water? Maybe you first did in a pool on vacation, with a friend's arms underneath you so you could feel weightless while staring up at the sky? It's an incredible feeling, and I have to give props to whoever thought up delivering that experience as a spa treatment in the form of sensory deprivation floating with enough magnesium to make you float in 12 inches of water and feel buoyant, but the water is room temperature, and there is no sound, and when you close the chamber door, you are enshrouded in darkness. Sound creepy? If you give it a try, maybe you'd come to the same conclusion. It feels a lot like how I'd imagine it is to be in outer space, just peacefully floating (obviously free of any meteor shower or disruption).

I floated and felt like I was in the cosmos. I lay there for probably ten minutes, but it felt infinite and timeless all at once. I considered my soul and spiritual journey.

I had to admit, I was damned proud of myself for making it months doing two hours. I was proud of how I'd relaxed my expectations of my two hours, and I just let it unfold, surrendering to the reality that I could never know the destination of this life, and that trying to control it brought so much stress to my peaceful inner being.

This exploration was the bulk of my first year of taking two hours. I geeked out on spiritual development during this time. If I spent two hours a day for one year, that's about 730 hours in total, and I honestly spent about 500 of those just hiking and walking and freeing my mind to wander and wonder about God, religion, and the parts of spirituality I hadn't sorted out for myself.

If the average Christian attends church for one hour a week, that's like spending almost ten years going to church. Damn. I said it. I'm like a decade into my spiritual journey in a year. Only this time, instead of being told what to think through a sermon, I was set free to just think and come to my own conclusions.

And I did just that. The bulk of my entire year and a half was spent sorting out my soul, my purpose, and who God or Source was to me. During that time, I went from an angry ex-Christian to a spiritually-sensitive intuitive who still loves Jesus. I credit how I spent my two hours to how that all unfolded. After a year, most of which was spent thinking deeply about what I really believed and listening to my inner wisdom to guide me, I had clarity.

CONCLUSION

What I've concluded is that I am so much happier, life is so much more magical, and my decisions are so much wiser since investing in my spirituality. I am less judgmental. I am more willing to believe multiple truths can coexist. I am happy for my Christian friends who genuinely have found God in their churches. I've confronted my fear of rejection with both sides of my family and been met with a variety of responses, and you know what, I give my parents credit. They showed me unconditional love when we really got into the depths of just how different my beliefs are.

Because here is my truth. There is no one path to God. No special people. No framework to have to get right to make it out of this life.

While religion may make you choose a way and give you an ultimatum, spirituality does not.

Regardless of what your religion is, you must be able to find guidance within you, or you cannot be free.

It's okay to not have all the answers and be on a quest for truth. This should be encouraged by all religious people. If you don't question what you believe, then you're afraid of being wrong. Any group that says you can't think for yourself and you need to follow a strict set of rules made for people at a different time than you in a different society than yours is putting a square peg into a round hole. The only way it works is for people to think so little of themselves that they don't care that they are being pushed into a round hole because they think something is so wrong with them that they deserve to be pounded into a round hole. That's not what I want from spirituality.

People don't need to be saved. Plenty of people are happily living in their religion and feel close and connected to God. God doesn't need people to waltz in and save other people. They need people to connect to the truth that resonates with them, expand into their potential, and enjoy living in that way. Believe that if something didn't work for you (religion wise), you'd move on and find what does because your soul wouldn't give you peace. Don't worry about anyone else. Trust that they will find what works for them and just go find what works for you.

And wouldn't that make for a happier, less hostile humanity?

What I now know about spirituality is that shedding the expectations and rigid framework of how I experienced religion was perhaps the best thing I ever did for my well-being. To step out from "the way it's supposed to be" into the land of "how it can be" is so life giving.

My relationship to my soul is truly sacred to me. I truly feel like I'm a soul having a human experience. My ability to connect through my gifts to God, while may not be as "on demand" as I'd like, is always a true gift to me. I feel like my spirit is untethered and free to fly where it needs.

That being said, what I've come to learn and respect is that everyone experiences God or the Universe in their own way, in their own time, and on their own terms. As a TikTok video just reminded me of today, "My capacity to allow other people to live a truth completely opposite of mine, without shutting off my compassion for them, is a reflection of how powerful my love is."

What I'm playing with right now when it comes to spirituality is:

I'm not trading one system for another. I'm clear that I'm not joining up with the spiritual community as a replacement for Christianity, which has just as many rituals, gurus who hurt people, and power dynamics as popular religions of the day. Nope, that's like trading one house for another with different paint, when I could live in a kickass tree house instead.

So the path I'm taking is the narrow one. It's a path free of precedent in a traditional sense, perhaps more solitary and less community around it, but it's mine., and I believe my soul knows its way home, and how that unfolds is part of the joy I get to uncover.

I still love Jesus and am focusing on the shared values and beliefs I do have with my Christian family members and friends. I think the danger of soulful shifts like I've gone through is to spend more time discussing and defending what you do not agree with, rather than acknowledging the shared parts that you do. At its core, I share many many beliefs with the Christian community and still have a true love for Jesus. I choose to focus on that.

I gave up needing to be understood by my Christian friends and family. A recovering people pleaser, I wanted so badly to be accepted by the people I grew up with and love so they could understand how amazing this journey has been for me, but not everyone has been excited to hear about it, because as I spoke about my spiritual liberation, the message they heard was that I had chosen a pathway to hell instead of salvation. It was like a complete disconnect, or in one case turned into an entire group of adults not speaking to me for days on end because they disapproved of my new beliefs. I went into full empathic distress, and it was the exact memory that popped into my head when I saw a meme that read "Ain't no hate like Christian love." Even if not intended as hate, no outsider would look at that and say, "Yep, that's love right there. Stoning someone with silence." What I'm exploring now is how can I love someone who seems committed to misunderstanding me? And how can I do that in love and kindness, while holding my boundaries? I may not have the answer now, but I'm actively discovering how to approach this.

I am releasing the need to fix anyone with a different faith experience than me. It's one of the hardest parts to trying to live peacefully alongside evangelical Christians. The constant need to "speak truth" into my life and try to correct me into a better path has felt so yucky to me. Because of that, it's my desire not to return the favor and try to influence others when they aren't asking me for my thoughts or experience.

chapter 12
NOT SO FEMININE

"She's got some fences, alright, but you just gotta hop over 'em."
- Ted Lasso

4 WEEKS TAKING TWO:
Adding One More Picture To the Fridge

I was late. Classic.

Rushing around the house, trying to locate my sock, and fielding the barrage of questions that inevitably get leveled at me right before I leave.

"Mommy, who's coming home first?"

"Paden, what do you want the kids to have for lunch? I think you're out of cucumber and hummus."

"Mama, can we go to the green park when you get back from work?"

"Also, I have a dentist appointment. Can you be home a little earlier today?"

Then my daughter opened a cupboard full of memorabilia, and it slipped right onto the floor. Bummer.

I quickly gathered it and pushed it back into the cupboard, feeling frustrated at how hard it is to get out of the house. Then a sweet little picture fell into my hand. It was my school picture, age six, looking so innocent and sweet. I couldn't bear to put it back in the cupboard.

Put it on the fridge, so when you see it, you remember to speak kindly to your inner child.

Good call, I thought. I put it on the fridge and made it out of the house in one piece.

I got in the car and thought about that picture. It felt significant because it brought me back to that powerful inner child healing I'd done in the Red Rocks of Sedona, and I drove to a pretty trailhead. My mind drifted to a conversation I had with my Dad the summer before I collapsed on the kitchen floor. He said something I'll never forget.

I asked him what I was like as a little girl. He simply said, "There was always one word that comes to mind when I think of you as a child. Kindness. You were the picture of kindness to everyone you met." That hit me in two ways.

I felt touched by his choice of words. I felt proud of that little girl. Kindness is an incredibly pure and beautiful quality to have. And then I felt crushed because I didn't think anyone would use that word to describe me now.

What the hell happened to me?

Would anyone use that word to describe me now?

Sadness welled up inside of me. I felt so far removed from the word kindness.

I thought back on my life and concluded, I have always had two parts to me. One side soft, kind and caring. One side driven, logical, and uncompromisingly strong. I saved one for business and one for my close inner circle … and operated like a light switch going through life deciding which side should show up.

Was I always like this, or was this just the aftermath of realizing as a child how burdensome it is to feel all the feelings and walk around carrying everyone's pain. Had I just found a way to cope and tried to harden myself up to block my absorption of others' feelings?

I hiked and pondered. I couldn't decide which was more true.

It's too hard to be an empath and feel everyone's feelings. Even if it has its own strength, the world doesn't value it, and to succeed, you don't need to soften; you need to harden. It was hard feeling everyone's feeling, and I hadn't seen sensitivity valued enough to want to learn to live with it. So was it any surprise that I bottled that side of me up for the last two decades?

I still didn't know what to do about it.

2 MONTHS TAKING TWO: That Time I Paid a Pack Rat Intuitive to Teach Me About Femininity

I fell in love with San Luis Obispo on my first hike up Bishop's Peak. So one morning during my time, I decided to hike to the top. Top to bottom it was an hour and a half, no breaks. I had just enough time.

As I scrambled over some small boulders on the zig zag path to the top, I thought about the Red Rocks of Sedona again and how much I'd hated the desert before that trip. Now it's one of the most beautiful places to me. It's funny how perspectives can change.

This got me thinking about a session I'd had in Sedona that I haven't shared here. It kicked off with me being invited into what looked like a hoarder's living room full of random-ass shit that you'd only find hopping from garage sale to garage sale for years. From floor to ceiling, long shelves were littered with odds and ends, figurines and dolls that may or may not come alive at night.

I was told to let my intuition guide me to something that I felt expressed my feminine energy. That was it - all the direction I was given. I didn't even know what intuition was at this point. Was my ear supposed to start twitching or my hands start heating up when I was close, like a giant game of cosmic hot and cold? Or were figurines supposed to start glowing so I'd find them?

I had no idea. I just kept wandering around to see what would happen.

After a very painful fifteen minutes of second guessing myself, finally I picked a figurine of a beautiful woman cradling a lamb like a child with a fierce lion walking beside her. There wasn't a particular reason why, outside of the fact that I just liked her.

The intuitive smiled, "Oh I see you're drawn to balancing both the divine feminine and divine masculine energies."

I had no idea what she was talking about then, so I nodded like I knew what the hell that meant, and clearly she picked up on my fake response, so she broke it down for me.

"Feminine energy and masculine energies aren't gendered energies. We all possess both in different amounts. When we overuse one side beyond our natural design, we throw the balance off, and it impacts us physically and emotionally. I sense that you've atrophied your gentle, intuitive feminine side and have relied far too long on your masculine need for results and competition."

I instantly thought about my unceremonious face plant in my kitchen, and the time my brother had called to recommend I start watching a show called "Yellowstone" because one of the characters reminded him of me right away - Beth. I thought it was a compliment until I watched the show and felt shocked that that ruthless woman reminded my brother of me. As unflattering as it was, I knew it represented something true: I'd been out of balance for a while. Sure, it was a large part of my career success, but it was also part of why I was so unhappy.

We moved on into what drew me to that specific figure and what meaning we could make. Here is what I learned. There is no one way to be female. There are many different facets to it. A women knows how to hold her innocence and gentleness close, as seen by the lamb, all the while never forgetting her strength and power, as seen by the lion.

And what I admitted in that session was that if being the truest expression of female is to equally represent or have equal access to both gentleness and strength, I was out of balance in my life. I remember leaving the session emotionally drained and confused about how my femininity was being expressed and how it was out of balance.

4 MONTHS TAKING TWO:
The Role that I Finally Got Celebrated for My Sensitivity

I sat once again in my car, freezing. Today I opted to meditate in the shelter of my car. I did a meditation, and my mind kept picturing Kennedy and my inner child as friends both with fire in us. To be honest, it didn't feel too revolutionary because I knew we both shared a very strong, fiery personality.

I started to stare out the window, watching the birds look for food, and I let my mind wander.

I pegged my firstborn's warrior energy early. Her fierceness. Her stubbornness. It's amazing how quickly we label characteristics in our kids, desperate to figure their little personalities out.

But I was in for quite a shock because while my confirmation bias was holding strong for the first eighteen months of her life, it wasn't until we took her to church that I started to sense something different.

I thought back to a Sunday a couple of years earlier. Michael wanted to go to church, and while I wasn't the biggest fan of church at that point, I was excited about putting Kennedy in free childcare for an hour to have adult thoughts and let my mind wander during the sermon. We found the toddler Sunday school room, signed her in, and they gave me a number. They told me if she needed me or was crying too hard for them to comfort her, that number would flash next to the stage, and I should keep an eye out, so if it flashed her number, I could come and get her.

I sat down. Happy to be kid free. They had started the announcements when it started flashing.

Oh shit, are you serious?

Yep, 1765.

Her number.

I bolted out of my seat and rushed to the room, where I collected a sobbing Kennedy.

"What happened?" I asked, worried.

"We don't really know. Little Jake hit his head on the slide and started to cry. Kennedy started to cry and hasn't been able to stop. Jake stopped, and we haven't been able to console her.

She was crying uncontrollably. I finally had to take her to the dark nursing room, neatly tucked away from the congregation, before she calmed down.

This was odd, I thought. It was like she had absorbed the distress of that little boy and couldn't get rid of it. Couldn't she distinguish her feelings from someone else's? I mean, that's what they say about empaths. Was Kennedy an empath?

Hmmm. She was certainly very sensitive to her environment, like that one time a fire engine went past us blaring its horn. She startled, screaming at the loud noises, clearly traumatized. And she's been sensitive to people, like that one time I was upset our neighbor had his landscapers dump all the dirt from their yard onto my front yard. She'd picked up on my tone of voice and burst into tears in the other room. Had she just absorbed the feelings of this little boy? Did she believe them to be her feelings?

From this point on, I watched her around other people.

I took note that when I got heated on a phone call, trying to rebook a plane flight, that she burst into tears, and I instantly hung up, feeling guilty. When she started daycare, her teachers told me every time she mirrored the emotions of the kids around her, feeling their feelings with them. She was incredibly drawn to animals. She calmed down instantly being outside.

Not knowing what a Highly Sensitive Person was (yet), something I would conclude about her later, I realized that my fiercely independent daughter was also a very compassionate empath.

And a very wise inner knowing stirred in me. *You are too.*

Me? No way.

I'm the one they call in to fire people in the office because I can do it and move on with my day.

I'm the one who gets uncomfortable when someone cries in front of me, far more comfortable with logic than hysterics.

I hadn't really identified with being an empath. Then a thought dropped in. *Yes, you have always been. You just didn't feel safe to express it, so you built walls around yourself to protect yourself. You didn't see any reward for being this way, so you hid your gift and overdeveloped others.*

Woah. Was that true? I wasn't sure. But one thing was for certain, becoming a mother had reopened doors in my heart I had long closed.

I sat there in my car thinking about that. Heading into Sedona on my soul adventure, I'd known Kennedy was an empath, but I didn't identify as one myself until after. Since then, she's been a huge teacher for me on how to balance two sides: strength and gentleness.

5 MONTHS TAKING TWO:
The Meditation That Had Me Frolicking
Down the Hillside, Arms Waving in the Air

By this time, I was really seeking new meditations and ways to explore this time alone. I knew I needed to be in nature, but I also liked peaceful meditations, so I stumbled upon a genre called "walking meditations."

(Aside: If you have never liked sitting still, this is where to start with meditation. Moving meditations can be as powerful!)

I typed into YouTube Divine Feminine walking meditation. Too narrow a search? Nope! YouTube delivered, o rather Rising Higher Meditation's channel did. A thirty-minute walking meditation sounded perfect to make it up the steep hill next to our house.

I was excited. I'd been drawn to the phrase Divine Feminine since the first time I heard it. Because for as much as society was trying to convince us all that women were equally valued, I was pretty jaded on how often I experienced the gap.

You know, the gender bias shit that makes you feel like someone accidentally took a page out of Mad Men and decided to role play in 2022.

Like watching my Mom, who loves to pray for other people, not be allowed to pray in a public church in Fresno, California because she was a woman, or the time I was a youth group leader but had to suffer listening to the male youth pastor discuss female modesty to our high schoolers. I had to listen to him mansplain to us all how women shouldn't tempt men with their clothing and should take responsibility for their part in sexual tension. I even told him ahead of this that he shouldn't be the one to talk to young women about their bodies, and he flat out dismissed me. I was a woman. My role was to support.

One of the things that drew me to spirituality early on was the reverence and sacredness given the feminine. It was damned refreshing to be honest. To be honored for more than motherhood. In a world that truly values the feminine, there is no need to rise up and fight to be valued or have a seat at the table. The spiritual community seemed to know there was deep sacred wisdom that women uniquely possessed. For the first time, I understood why women had been the muses of artists since the dawn of time.

Twenty minutes into this peaceful walking meditation, the lovely Australian voice had me imagining I was riding on a beautiful horse in an open field. I was literally walking in an open field. No one was around me, so when her voice guided me to the sensation of feeling alive and riding a horse with my hands stretched up to the heavens, I totally fell in line. I went full role play, and started galloping in the meadow with my arms stretched out and my face smiling into the sunshine. I felt a childlike joy, and it was incredible.

After that experience, which I repeated many many times, I started to associate being female with being revered, holding deep wisdom, the seat of intuition, the free, creative side that longs to be a muse.

But that was just the beginning.

SIX MONTHS TAKING TWO:
The Time I Unleashed My Inner List
Writer and Did a Deep Dive

When I started to take two hours a day, I imagined it would reduce my stress and bring joy into my life because I was playing again. I could never have expected that daily decompressing would facilitate a complete personal rebrand on being feminine. I started to realize how conflicted I was about what side of being female was the most important and natural side of me.

One day, during my two hours, I drove twenty minutes to a really beautiful lookout point next to the ocean. I tuned in to Aubrey Marcus' podcast (again) about the balance of feminine and masculine energy. I learned that there is a far more expansive view of the feminine and the masculine. It's not a gendered grouping of traits, rather it is a spectrum that we each uniquely play in regardless of gender. Each side has a divinely expressed side and a wounded side.

He started to go through a list of what the divine feminine was and what the wounded feminine was, and I pulled the car over because I'm a notorious note-taker, and I wrote down this list:

WOUNDED FEMININE	HEALTHY FEMININE
Insecure and needy	Intuitive
Needy, approval seeking	Grounded
Codependent	Magnetic
Manipulative	Empathetic
Inauthentic	Strong
Overly sensitive, emotional	Boundaries
Victim	Creative
Blaming others	Open
Chases love	Vulnerable
Desperation	Receptive
Demanding	Flows with life
Passive aggressive	Supportive

No sense of self	Receptive and confident in her body
Smothering	Playful
Sacrificing herself for others	Connected
Oversharing	Asks for what she needs
No boundaries	Enjoys process of creation
Overwhelmed	Community builder

I saw myself all over both sides of the list. No real surprise there. But what I found myself in awe of was the healthy feminine side. I mean, that is one badass woman right there. She wasn't weak or anyone's doormat. I could envision her as a mother, CEO, and a President. Those traits demanded so much respect. I highlighted the qualities I knew I possessed and underlined the ones I wanted to have more of:

Intuition

Boundaries

Grounded energy

Flows with life

Enjoys the process of creation

I turned the podcast back on, and Aubrey Marcus dove into the masculine side, and I scribbled quickly:

WOUNDED MASCULINE	HEALTHY MASCULINE
Controlling	Vision
Domineering	Loves structure and logic
Aggressive	Honest and accountable
Cold & distant	Protector
Withdraws from love	Initiates
Avoids	Provides clear direction
Too Competitive	Adventure

Abusive	Purpose
Unstable	Stable
Over thinking, brooding	Clarity
Punishing, judgmental	Witnesses, no judgment
Unable to ask for help	Integrity and awareness
Insensitive	Deeply present
Impatient	Outcome focused
Defensive of self	Committed and powerful
No direction	Decisive
Fear of failure	Focus and discipline
Needs to be right	Humble
Attachment to success	Grounded and of service

And there again, I saw myself all over that list. I loved that list too. It was also deserving of respect, and what our world seems to have completely forgotten is that the healthy masculine doesn't compete with the healthy feminine. They complement each other. More than that, the healthy masculine needs the healthy feminine, something the business world has yet to acknowledge and why I was struggling to realize my own leadership potential.

Was it weird that I saw myself in both lists? Was I half and half?

A brand new thought darted into my mind:

You are both the ice and the fire. The art and the science. The giver and receiver. You have both sides in you. When balanced, they dance together. When not, they are not at war.

War. That felt right. I had a war going on inside. That much was clear, and I knew deep in my soul that once I balanced them, I would be at peace and could step into a much more natural version of myself.

I parked the car and went up the mountain. I had been at war for a long time about how to show up in this world, how to stand in my power, and how to bring balance to both sides of me. I saw for the first time that I wanted to cultivate both sides of me and be able to pull from the side that was most appropriate for each situation, without having to be so damn compartmentalized and, basically, lead a double life.

EIGHT MONTHS TAKING TWO: Polarization Is Healthy

I spent months wandering and wondering about what it is to step into the healthy traits of the feminine and the masculine. I focused more at work on how to bring in my intuition. I asked more questions during my two hours about how to lead, handle situations, and I got guidance. Every time I took it, it worked well. I learned how to balance my energy. Once I felt the difference and knew how good it felt, I did energy audits on myself. Over months I found certain methods that worked consistently. I paid attention to when there were signs that I was out of alignment and needed to rebalance my energy, mainly being able to pick out when I was coming from a place of wounding, not from a divine expression.

Most commonly it was:

- Feeling anger, when deep down it was just being hurt
- Building a wall of armor to protect myself
- Ignoring my body's cries to slow down and rest
- Disconnected from my body sexually
- Out of touch with my intuition
- Victim mode and harsh blaming others
- Need to control people and life so I can feel secure
- Feeling vindictive and wanting revenge

Whenever I did this, I'd go back to the list I was building on how to balance my energy, and I'd pick something that sounded fun.

- Energy healing from a healer
- Chakra balancing meditation

- Spending time outside in nature to ground and recharge
- Dance or sing out your intentions. I have a song I put on that I connect to manifesting, and as I listen to it, I call in with my body and words all the dreams I want to materialize.
- Go for a hike, put on spiritual music you love and sing/ hum along
- Dance to songs in C major or D major (connected to Root and Sacral Chakras) to balance and ground your energy in your lower chakras
- I AM meditations - meditate on all the divine feminine qualities you want to embody and state that as "I am compassionate. I am intuitive. I am flowing with life… etc."

And I felt more like myself and more integrated than ever before. I also felt more in control and less like a victim of a world that still is figuring all this out. I didn't have to wait for a leadHER to show up. I could start shifting to be that for myself, and in doing so, perhaps be a leadHER for others.

CONCLUSION

Once again, I was surprised by the breakthroughs gifted to me as a result of making space every day to just focus on BEING instead of DOING. Who knew that "Being" was more feminine and "Doing" was more Masculine? So part of my great undoing was to be a human being again. It actually meant embracing the healthy, feminine traits and valuing them. Doing that had me loving my sensitivity and seeing it like the superpower it is. I now loved tuning into other people's energy and sensing what wasn't being said. It felt like a sacred gift, one that couldn't exist without sensitivity, and I was seeing it pay off as a leader with managing people, in my marriage, as a mother, as a daughter, and friend. Over the course of the year, I saw my sensitivity come back into its fullness, and I reclaimed the side of me that had defined me as a child.

It was powerful. I felt liberated, and I navigated through my roles with more ease, intention, and divinity than before.

What I now know about being female is that it is sacred, it is powerful, and it wants to be unleashed. That femininity possesses deep magic. Ancient cultures revered the intuition of the feminine and gave her respect and positions of power. She was more than a mother. She sat not just at the tables, but in places of honor. As the world's consciousness wakens, the female energy has the power to bring peace to nations, kindness to board rooms, creativity to the void, and great healing to souls.

I now value the feminine around me and in me, and I've been playing more with stepping into the easeful flow available to us that is feminine energy, releasing masculine control and giving way to more ease, more play, and more alignment.

What I am exploring about the feminine is:

Trusting my intuition and tracking my batting average. I keep journals right now full of predictions, premonitions, spirit-filled messages and answers I receive for questions my friends ask me or I am seeking personally, and I track what comes to pass. This allows my left brain to align with the trust of my right brain. While I may have not manifested a lake house, I know a better one is coming at a more aligned time.

Embracing both sides of me and not ditching the masculine side. While I may have atrophied my feminine side for a long time, I stand now at around 50/50 split of both energies, and I love them both now. I see how an overdeveloped masculine wore me out physically, isolated me socially, and left me stewing in pent up frustration often. I don't try to reduce the masculine. I simply make way for the feminine. I focus on bringing her traits forward and letting her shine. This takes the heat off my masculine energy from carrying too much of the burden and blame. When the feminine is given space to expand, the masculine gets to rest.

[Side note: honestly, if we all reread this paragraph in light of gender equality and embraced it, I honestly think the balance we seek could be beautifully restored.]

Exploring my sensitivity. There is no doubt that once I embraced that I was a highly sensitive person and saw the power of sensitivity, the more I cultivated it. I even had a friend recently tell me that "you're so much more sensitive now, I'm worried I'm going to hurt your feelings." The truth I knew as soon as she said it was two fold:

- Careless or harsh words always hurt me, even before.
- I was not only allowing myself to feel it, but I was speaking up and letting those around me know how I now wanted to be treated in light of my sensitivity.

Breaking the cycle of self betrayal.

One of the symptoms of a dysfunctional feminine is over serving others at a cost to herself. My conditioning and modeling in this area has gone back decades. I am present to the cycle of guilt showing up and then people pleasing, or self-betrayal patterns coming in to reduce my guilt. This could be in overcommitting at work, saying too many "yes's" to things I don't actually want to do, like social events or in performing in sex when my mind is elsewhere. All violations of my truth. I no longer believe anyone's approval of me is worth sacrificing my own approval, but that being said, it's a constant awareness that is growing inside of me.

In therapy it was called codependent. As a trauma response, it's called fawning, and in plain English, it's a habit of depleting and denying yourself by putting everyone else's needs above yours. Taking two hours was one of the most profound ways I stepped out of this cycle and into prioritizing myself, but it continues to show up daily in corners and crevices of my life that I am uncovering.

If there's one ultimate takeaway it's that we are all navigating life. We can cope, suppress, mask, or we can evolve and grow our way through it. It all comes down to how willing you are to question yourself, witness the discomfort of dysfunction, and be willing to stick with incremental shifts that chart their way to improvement.

PART 3

The Transformation

"In surrender, you no longer need ego defenses and false masks,
you become very simple, very real"
- Eckhart Tolle

There is a time in every journey that affords you a view that just takes your breath away. You may plot along over time making small adjustments, but at some point you'll turn around and witness your progress. It will take your breath away. And when it does, it's time to celebrate it.

But progress is one thing. Coming back to a similar place and viewing it completely different isn't about appreciating a new landscape. It's about applauding the shift in perspective, honoring the changes, celebrating the new eyes you have to see and experience the world around you.

chapter 13
UNCOVERING PEACE

"You know what the happiest animal on Earth is? It's a goldfish. You know why? It's got a 10-second memory. Be a goldfish."
- Ted Lasso

I have one more profound shift I made during the almost two years of taking two hours a day. To do that, I want to take you back to 2019.

If you're a business leader, you know how powerful having a clear vision is. It's the thing that unites your team, inspires everyone to push hard because the goal is so important. In 2019 we hit every goal we had ever put into a vision. We were at an all-time high and so uncomfortable with it. I'll never forget when Michael admitted to me, "I have everything I ever wanted. Is that bad?" That's when we started to get restless.

We were hustlers, grinding out work. Happy to run a marathon like sprinters, crushing that old traditional "hard work is the only path to success" model. I mean, in the first five years of our marriage, we didn't take a single vacation longer than a three-day weekend. We watched our friends buy better cars, bigger homes, and feel so much pressure to earn more because their standard of living was so steep. We felt proud of the fact that we could live happily with $50k per year in California. It gave us total flexibility to pour every dollar the business made as profit, back into the business. Frugal and hustle doesn't even begin to describe our lives. Let's just say no one wanted our lives for those early years.

By 2019 we saw the payoff, and when I asked Michael what was next, he looked blankly at me and said, "I have no idea. I've reached every one of my goals." That didn't sit well with either of us. Michael had to dream bigger, and I was finally about to put into words for the first time how resentful I was that I'd spent the greater part of a decade learning how to help entrepreneurs bring their ideas to market, and yet I hadn't even asked myself what my dreams were. Which, of course, was just one more way self-betrayal had shown up in my life. So we signed up for Tony Robbins and Dean Graziosi's Knowledge Business Broker course, a course that blends marketing with some of Tony's best personal development exercises. That for us created one of the most profound realizations I'd had.

One of the exercises we did was called Seven Layers Deep. It's a series of asking yourself why you want to be successful and drilling into the deepest purpose behind your drive for success. Here's what mine looked like:

Level 1: Why do you want to be successful in life?

Because I never want to feel poor again.

Level 2: Why is it important to you to never be poor?

Because life becomes stressful and relationships get strained.

Level 3: Why is it important to you to avoid stress and strained relationships?

It takes the color out of life and makes me want to retreat.

Level 4: Why is it important to you for life to be filled with color and not want to retreat from it? *Because I want to experience everything good this life can offer.*

Level 5: Why is it important to you to experience everything good this life can offer?

Because I only get one shot at life and I want to enjoy it.

Level 6: Why is it important to you to enjoy life?

Because it brings me happiness and satisfaction.

Level 7: Why is it important to you to be happy and satisfied?

Then I will feel that I lived my life to its fullest and find peace.

I was so shocked by this final answer. It was the first time in my life I'd ever identified the word peace as close to a goal, much less the driving goal of my life. I wouldn't ever have guessed that the chase I was on wasn't about success or money; it was about peace and contentment. I felt disoriented for a few minutes. The answer didn't feel like me, and honestly, I almost started the exercise over, hoping to "do better next time."

But then I sat with it and thought about it.

I remembered each time I gave birth and had to visualize something that could anchor my mind during the struggle of pushing a baby the size of a watermelon out of my your vagina. I always pictured a beach I visited in Tulum, Mexico with the beautiful blue ocean water and a graceful palm tree with coconuts, its thick branch beckoning me to sit on it like a swing, as nature sang to me. In every critical moment in my life, when I desperately needed something to believe in to hold on to, I daydreamed about being in nature, surrounded by beauty. For me this is the embodiment of peace.

Maybe I'd always wanted peace.

That started to feel more and more true, and that meant I needed to acknowledge I was way off course. Because anyone looking at my work ethic, driving ambition, and big dreams, couldn't possibly conclude I was in pursuit of peace.

But my soul was.

I wanted a life of ease, flow, peace, and contentment. And like so many, I'd bought the belief that the ONLY way to achieve that was to work hard enough early on to afford the ability to slow down and breathe at the end of your life. So that became the plan.

I was obsessed with hustle, always sprinting, no time for rest, overwhelmed and drowning in tasks. I felt like someone who was trying to navigate through a jungle so I could see a beautiful waterfall, only to realize when I looked at how my GPS was directing me, I was really en route to a precipice. I could feel deep down that that was the soul-tugging sensation I'd been feeling all year. I was not on the right path. I had to course correct. If I wanted peace, my life needed to map towards that, and just chasing the $40 million dollars I thought I needed to be happy, didn't make much sense. When your goal is peace, how much money do you really need to achieve that?

I wasn't sure. So the next time Michael and I went to our wealth advisors to get an update on our net worth and define our vision for the future, I laid it out.

"How much money do I need to be able to live until ninety-six, be able to have $120k per year in income, and have zero dollars left in the bank when I pass? Without including the sale of two homes, which would be the only assets I wanted to hand down or sell in the scenario that we lived past our mid-nineties?"

God, they loved me. Kidding. They looked at me like I was crazy. No one in the history of their practice ever asked for that financial scenario. But I did. I did it because deep down I had to know what number I was chasing. So the next visit they told me it wasn't $40 million I needed but was more like $6 million, and we were on track to hit that by age fifty

My mind was blown. What a massive difference $6 million was compared to $40 million. Think of all the years of hard work we just saved by actually mapping out the end game. That was so powerful for me and a HUGE insight into one simple truth: you don't need to have tens of millions of dollars to have peace. You don't need to wait until you are seen as a success by the world to learn how to be at peace.

This clarified for me a huge tug of war I experienced almost daily. I had bought into the great American lie: More is better. But more is not necessarily better. It all depends on what you have more of. More responsibilities is not necessarily better. More stress is not better. More of a house is not necessarily better if you have to work harder or get a side gig going to afford it. I didn't need more of that, and yet that's the kind of more I was chasing.

But what became clear to me was that I needed more time to relax. I needed more playfulness. More thinking time. More creativity. More exploration. More time with my loved ones. That's the kind of more I needed.

And that didn't need money to achieve.

I had thought that I needed more "success," more wealth, and more influence to achieve my dreams, when what I really needed was to stop doing more and start focusing on how to be a person of peace, truly content with what I already had.

I decided to only say YES to things that bring or promise to bring more peace into my life.

And then life heated up for me. I had a second baby, got postpartum depression, was consumed with helping Michael build a second business, and then the pandemic hit and my world spun upside down.

I forgot about peace. I forgot about contentment. When you're in survival mode, finding peace and contentment in the midst of battle will only come to you from muscle memory - not will power.

Muscle memory comes from discipline and consistency. Which I found through my two hours.

I started my two hours a day not to get more peace back in my life but to avoid getting a full blown autoimmune disease. I did it to *not* lose my mind. I did it to save myself from living a life I wanted to escape from. And after doing it for a full year and a half, it became clear to me that once again my soul had intervened and pulled me back from my default mode of running toward that cliff and had rerouted me back to that beautiful waterfall.

Taking two hours a day gave me the framework I needed to actually invite peace and contentment into my life. I was so focused on getting two hours in each day that it worked. Every time I did, I felt more at peace, more content with myself and my life. And I have to believe it has something to do with being so goal oriented about just carving out those hours. I was focused on the mechanics of fitting two hours into each day. That became my sole focus.

It's the very thing I'd missed in my personal development journey.

Too often we hear phrases like "be happy" or "be at peace," and it honestly annoyed the hell out of me. It was too vague. I was too detached from my spirit to truly know what specific activity or thing I could consistently do to bring me genuine and predictable happiness or peace. It felt too undefined.

But the gift of taking two hours is that I was so focused on finding that specific amount of time each day that I was no longer focused on finding peace. Finding peace is like chasing a moving target, but finding two hours was possible. That became in and of itself a chase. It was something I could check a box with, and it's why it worked. I checked that damned box 360 times in a year.

But the transformation didn't come from the box checking. It came from what happened to me when I stepped into a void of time each day. All I had to do was to step into that two hours to find peace and happiness. It was that simple and profound. Just having that much time to do whatever the hell I wanted brought more happiness and peace to my life than anything else I've ever done.

And here's the joke. I've meditated for years. I've written for a local magazine about every hiking trail in town. I've done all the self-care services you could imagine, but it never had the same impact or the sense of calm that walking into a two-hour window of time with no expectations, no pressure, and know I could have laid down in the grass and sunshine for two full hours, gotten a hideous sunburn, and still walked away happy and overflowing.

And it all comes down to one profound distinction.

Self-love and self-care aren't about doing, they're about being. Peace isn't something you do; it's a state of being.

My whole life I have been caught in a spiral of burning hot and bright and then getting snuffed out with burnout, only to repeat it again and again. What was I missing? What does a flame need consistently to keep burning sustainably? Oxygen. That was what I'd never been able to consistently supply myself with, and as someone who for thirty-four years of life was obsessed with being a human doing, taking two hours to just be was the breath of fresh air I needed. It was the oxygen I had been seeking.

I believe we don't need one more thing to do. We need time to practice just being. Being free from distraction. Free from pressure. Free from expectation. Free from judgement. We need time to be free to explore. Free to expand. Free to process. Free to wonder. Free to find. And free to discover who we really are and to come back to our true essence.

And I found that by taking two hours, I found my way back to peace, and I found it long before I found my $6 million dollars and could retire.

chapter 14
A LOT CAN CHANGE IN A YEAR

"If you would have told me that I'd be drinking tea at 3 o'clock every day, about a year ago... I would have punched you in the mouth."
- Ted Lasso

I love when a picture I took a year before shows up on my phone. When you have kids, particularly, it's incredible to look back at your 2-year-old and remember that only a year before when they could barely walk.

One unexpected lesson to me during the pandemic was how incredible it is to measure time by the ages of my friends' kids, particularly with the limited contact many of us had during the outbreak. I remember one of my friends had her baby the week before California went into lockdown, and the first time I saw her little girl, she was already walking and climbing by herself up jungle gyms and sliding down slides by herself.

Growth is so easy to measure when you see it through the lens of children's height, capabilities, and the way their look dramatically changes. We can anticipate big changes in a couple of scenarios or milestone events in our lives. One of those is when you leave home for the first time. You've spent something like eighteen years with the same people, navigating familiar, repetitive situations, and you understand the relational dynamics really well. Then you go off to college, and you're thrown into a new environment with unfamiliar people who bring fresh, complicated dynamics and pressures into your orbit, which you must navigate alone. It's a huge period of growth. Then you go home for Christmas or summer break, and it feels earth shattering. Everyone expects you to walk in the same person that left a few months before for college, and you think they should all be in step with how you've evolved.

And while we come to expect that in kids, when did we start expecting adults to remain the same person year over year? I may be the outlier here, but one of my goals is to be in constant iteration so that when people come into contact with me after not seeing me for a year, there's a definite shift that's noticeable.

When I started taking two hours a day to restore my soul, I felt:

- Burned out, depleted in my daily life
- Exhausted, and my energy crashed daily
- Self-conscious about my broken out face
- Insecure over weight gain
- Emotionally reactive
- Depressed
- Anxious daily and afraid of dropping any ball
- Controlling, needing to know everything and responsible for anything slipping through the cracks
- Mildly interested in sex, but having it so I could tell myself my relationship was okay
- Resentful about my career
- Resentful that my kids were so little, needy, and inconvenient to my daily goals
- Focused on finding what wasn't working, what was broken, and what wasn't ideal in all areas of my life

- Desperate to be positive and giving myself pep talks to try to snap out of it, but it was a daily battle
- Critical of what I accomplished and how quickly (never good enough or quickly enough) In denial about how stressed out I was because I had normalized my chronic overwhelm
- Impatient for my dreams to show up for me
- Annoyed that the hard work I'd done on so many areas of my life wasn't working out like I'd hoped.
- Discouraged because my attempts to lift myself weren't sustainable
- Distant from my soul and from God

And as I write this, almost two years later, I am still imperfect. I still ride roller coasters of emotions and circumstances, but it's significantly less frequent, and when it does happen, my batting average to recover myself has vastly improved.

Overall, I'd say my life now feels:

- Energized and inspired.
- Consistent energy each day, even without drinking coffee anymore.
- Reduced stress and clear skin.
- Most of the time I'm happy with how my body looks, and I'm proud of all it has done to support me and the wisdom it holds.
- Emotionally equipped to respond with kindness, except that one time family members didn't talk to me and froze me out for three days and we were snowed in and I couldn't escape. I'll give myself a hall pass for that. (That was insane.)
- Balanced, despite what's on my plate. I now choose to believe that whatever needed to get done did and the rest can wait. I'm free of believing I am so necessary.

- Trusting that I will be supported by my team to get done what needs to and if something slips, we'll be fine.
- Excited about sex, and I'm the initiator in our home, often waking my husband up in the middle of the night to have sex.
- Resourcefully charting a new career path, taking ownership for my dreams.
- Enjoying that my kids are adorable, demanding, but so stinking cute at ages two and four. Thankful that they are the biggest reason in my life to disengage with work and not become consumed with hustle. They are my reason for valuing balance.
- Celebrating what is going well, cultivating a thankful spirit and making generous assumptions where possible.
- Far more positive thinking and abundance mindset patterns are emerging than ever before.
- So damned proud of who I am and in love with the person I am becoming. I still see growth edges and areas I'd like to improve, but I focus on how exciting it will be to evolve into higher levels of consciousness.
- I set up boundaries around my time and my workload and have re-trained most people who work with me that I am not living to the beat of the same drum as before. Guess what? The business is still alive and the responsibilities have been shifted to more strategically aligned team players than me.
- Patient and expectant for my boldest dreams to show up for me. I've dreamt bigger and believe in my soul that the order has been placed, and it is all on its way. It's not a matter of IF; it's a matter of WHEN, which excites me.
- In full trust that all the hard work we put in and all the struggles we went through have made us who we are today, and I am so proud of the woman I am becoming.

- Tuned in and listening to my intuition to guide me on the path I'm walking. I don't see it all and that doesn't bother me now because the journey IS the destination. I wouldn't want to know every play-by-play of my life. How boring.
- Connected like never before to my soul and make time daily to connect to divine guidance and God
- … I'll add that I'm quick to apologize, when given the chance. I am less egotistical because I now feel called into service, and my ego is not as necessary to serve others. Exploring new things and unafraid to fail. I give more grace to myself when I don't show up the way I'd hoped. I love myself. Even as I acknowledge that thought, I may never be fully healed. I am healing.

How wild are these two lists? And this is just from the first year of doing this! I am so fucking proud of this shift in just one year.

Do you see why I can't imagine not taking my two hours?

Imagine who I will be in a decade if I keep carving out time for my soul to be restored and transform.

Imagine what two hours a day could mean for you?.If you just isolate the verbs of the above lists, it's even more dramatic. You'll get an even more bleak view of how it felt to live my 2020 life: burned out, depleted, exhausted, stressed, insecure, reactive, hiding, anxious, overwhelmed, afraid, controlling, disinterested, resentful, critical, desperate, critical, judgmental, denial, impatient, annoyed, trying, discouraged, distant.

But by 2021, here's how it felt to live my life: Energized, inspired, consistent, reduced stress, happy, proud, emotionally equipped, balanced, free, trusting, excited, resourceful charting, enjoying, valuing balance, celebrating, cultivating, generous assumptions, positive, abundant, in love, set up boundaries, patient, expectant, in full trust, tuned in, listening, connected, quick to apologize, less egotistical, exploring new things, unafraid, giving more grace, loving.

Looking back over the last year, two of the biggest takeaways for me have been the concepts of self-love and transformation. Self-love is the key to any transformation. You can't hate yourself enough to move into transformation. You can only love yourself as you are AND be excited for your progress into an even better version of who you can be. But it starts with love. The moment you finally love yourself is the minute you make peace with your past.

When people hear that I have a self-care practice, they assume it's spa treatments or working out all the time, getting a weekly massage or getting my hair or nails done. They always seem surprised to know it's simply a practice of making space in my soul to relax and focus on being. The truth is by taking two hours a day I got clarity of consciousness. I became a better mom. I became a lover of my own soul. I became a better lover. I set boundaries. I became a better friend who was supported by better friends. I stopped trying so hard to compete in a man's world and owned my feminine power. I healed from deep wounds. I reconnected with God. I learned to trust myself.

And I got the balls (or vagina) needed to document the good, bad, and the supernatural into a book. The goal in this book isn't to convince you of my viewpoints or truth, but to show you how being alone, prioritizing myself, and finding happiness had profound impacts on what I believed, who I became, and how the world rose up to meet me there.

> **People can change. *You* can change. I am proof of that.
> Let's look for it. And cheer for it.**

At the beginning of this book, if you recall, I was forced to face my brokenness, and all I wanted was to fix myself. That's where it started.

"I feel like shit and want to escape my life How can I fix that?" This journey didn't start with wanting to get to know myself. I wanted to get to know the fixed version, not the broken one.

But I had it all wrong. You don't fix yourself enough to actually love your own company. You have to learn to love yourself exactly as you are. You have to build trust with yourself. You have to extend love and forgiveness to yourself. You have to support and protect yourself. And only when you do this can you look back and see the healing that has taken place.

I love this meme I recently saw on Instagram:

"I love it when I realize I'm handling a situation better than my old self would have."

That's my new way of measuring growth and celebrating it. I didn't know that then. I only knew coming back from Sedona that I had been handed a prescription to do the very thing I was afraid of: spending time alone. And I did it, every day for a whole year, and so much shifted for me. This entire book is dedicated to the journey.

The truth is I almost didn't write this book because I didn't want to create a book that felt preachy or superior. So that's NOT the book you're holding right now. I am a BIG believer in not sharing advice. Weird, right? I mean, I'm a small business consultant who is literally paid to "give advice." But, nope. I share knowledge, intuition, and experience - not advice.

Here's why. I can't possibly understand what it is to be you. Period. I don't know what it's like to have lived your life, to have survived your life experience to this point. We could go out for coffee for two hours and you could tell me all your experiences to date, and I still wouldn't have a damn clue about what it feels like to be you, to think like you, to feel like you, to see the world like you.

So to honor that, this book is *not* advice. This book is my story. It's my lived experience, and I'm sharing a glimpse into that journey with you. If it resonates with you, inspires you, or triggers you, I trust that you will take only what serves you and leave the rest behind.

I don't have all the answers., and I acknowledge that I may not have the answer you bought this book to discover. I have who I am, what I did, and what lessons I derived from it. I trust you will be able to discern what is for you and use that to navigate your life.

That being said, many have asked how they can facilitate a similar journey for themselves in their own life, and when I share, I break down the mindset shifts and practical lessons I learned, which I truly believe set me up for more success.

FOUND TIME

The first thing I had to rethink was this notion that the stars would align and I'd magically have a welcoming, convenient, perfectly-timed opportunity to take two hours. Forget it. It never once happened like that for me. And plenty of times I ended up grabbing a 45-minute time slot and then getting another hour later in the day. So if I was starting out again, I'd rethink my concept of finding time. I'd give up on ever finding the time. You can find five minutes, sure, but not two hours.

You will have to decide if it's important enough to you to make time. And here's what I know, if a friend called me for help, I would make time. If my child needed me, I'd drop everything. If my sister was passing through town and wanted to stop by with the kids to see our family, we'd make time. No question. If a coworker's child was up sick and she'd barely slept four hours and couldn't finish her end of a project, I'd make time in my day to help finish the project. I'd rework my plans in the evening in a heartbeat and probably tell her it was no big deal and that I was happy to help.

I have a multi-decade track record of time making to help others. Beyond that, I have a long ancestral line that sacrificed self in service of others. It's so built into my DNA, I didn't know another way. It feels good, and it appeals to our inner heroes desire to be of service. It also fills our need to be needed.

But here's the catch. If I can make time for others, I'm a time maker. If I can show up for others when it's inconvenient, I've proven that I can show up when it's inconvenient. All of which means I can make time for myself. I can show up for myself when it's inconvenient. Unfortunately, just because I can doesn't mean I will. Which brings me to my next point.

TREAT YOURSELF LIKE YOUR BEST FRIEND

If I asked you to name all the things you love, how long would it take until you wrote down your own name?

If that hit you between the eyes, we're in the same boat. I first saw that on a social media thread and felt it so deeply. I can honestly say before this journey of taking two hours a day, it would have never occurred to me to write down my own name.

So often it's easy to *say* that I'm a priority, but if I ever needed a break, would I take it? If I needed to not show up for a family reunion one Christmas, for my own sanity, would I ask for it? If I needed to sleep more, would I take a nap? If I needed a girls' night out, would I initiate it? If I needed to tell a client that I don't respond to their calls on the weekends, could I set that boundary?

Saying "I am a priority" is one thing. Acting like it's true is completely foreign. And people vote with their feet, not their words. Follow actions,and you'll find what's in someone's heart. In a world that teaches us to sacrifice for others, especially as women, a big hurdle is actually treating yourself like a priority.

So there is no hack that I'm aware of, no secret trick to making this happen for you overnight. The only thing that has helped me is to stop acting like I'm no one's priority. Start telling yourself, "I am a priority." I reminded myself that the only person who is going to be there for me every day, who wakes up with me, journeys with me, laughs with me, and cries with me is ME. I am my own best friend, and it's time to start acting like it.

And I had to repeat phrases like that in my head on the way to work and write it down on sticky notes, and move its location frequently to keep it fresh in my mind.

I read that the average human brain thinks up to 64,000 unique thoughts per day. And 98 % of the time they are negative, recycled thoughts from the previous day. Only 2% of your thoughts are new and fresh to that day, so we sure as hell better intentionally place some good thoughts in there. So I've consciously been brainwashing myself with motivating reminders to love myself and that I deserve it.

STOP TRYING TO BE SO DAMN PRODUCTIVE

So once you decide you can make time, and that you're a real priority in your life, you'll probably start your two-hour journey like I did, damned proud that you actually did the thing and made time.

Then you'll sit there, all alone, and wonder, "Shit, what do I do now?"

And you'll likely start to think of things that are a hybrid of fun and productive. Warning to all my fellow productivity powerhouses: It has no place in your two hours. It's literally the main thing that gets in your way. One of the biggest blocks to creativity, happiness and playfulness is the compulsion to be productive at all times.

It's what I call cultural productivity compulsion. You know, that good old American need to always be doing something useful so that you can believe you are useful. In my experience, it will literally block you from the work you have to do here. It's one of the biggest differences between children and adults. Children can so easily abandon responsibilities and set fire to all the "have tos" in life and jettison right into happiness. It's a skill, it's a gift, and most of us have to rediscover this in our lives.

Redefine productivity.

Is it productive to give your mind a break from problem solving and multitasking all day?

Is it productive to rebalance your central nervous system so you're less reactive in life?

Is it productive to let your mind wander so you can discover new ideas or concepts?

Is it productive to enjoy yourself in the middle of the day, giving you renewed energy to kick even more ass during your day?

YES, every single time.

If you believe this to be true, internalize it, breathe it in, then let it go. When you finally give yourself permission to take a break from life, it won't feel productive. Expect it, embrace it, and know that when you look back, overtime, the results will come in, and it will be profound.

PAY ATTENTION TO YOUR SELF-CARE

Growing up, my Dad was notorious for prescribing H2O consumption for any of life's ailments. If you complained about a headache, he'd announce, "Dehydration!" If your stomach felt weird, he'd slide a glass of water over the table. It became a light-hearted joke. He was the King of Hydration.

We all know we should drink enough water during the day. If we don't drink ANY, we get symptoms. Which is why this book documents the profound shifts that can happen when you build a habit around daily soul maintenance, otherwise we end up waiting for it to get bad again before we pay attention, or like me, collapse on the kitchen floor.

So when it comes to identifying when you need self-care, one thing I know for sure is your body sends you signals well in advance of any crash or sickness. One of the skills I developed through this year was picking up on the signals.

Some of the signs your mental health is in need of a "time in" are:

- Your energy levels have decreased
- You snap at others
- Everything is starting to feel like a chore/work
- You feel trapped in a negative situation
- You struggle to engage in anything besides your current stressors
- You feel overwhelmed by your responsibilities
- You become more protective of your feelings/defensive
- You start escaping into your imagination/reliving "better times"
- You do more "mindless"/aimless activities than usual (e.g. excess TV)
- You get "hung up on"/triggered by things that normally wouldn't bother you
- Changes in sleep patterns
- You start prioritizing immediate pleasure/comfort over long term gain
- You start withdrawing from your friends/loved ones
- You avoid making plans in the future because you feel your state/mood is unpredictable
- You struggle to get pleasure/joy/stress relief out of the things you used to do

If any of the above connects to where you are in your life as you read it, the Depression Project suggests prioritizing self-care, and I hope this book helps you start to envision what that could look like for you.

(Source: The Depression Project)

Why we aren't taught this in school baffles me because learning this now has been so profound.

RETURNING TO SELF-LOVE ISN'T SOMETHING YOU NEED TO LEARN

I also don't want this book to be used to validate a misconception that, I think, holds a lot of us back from truly experiencing self-love. Self-care isn't the path to self-love. You don't go from not loving yourself to going on hikes outside and loving yourself. That's not the prescription for self-love. In some cases, that's just more checking the box to feel like you did show yourself love. But here's the thing, loving yourself originates somewhere else.

The path to healing is not learning to love yourself. Contrary to popular opinion, you ARE love, as you are. If you did nothing new, you'd still be pure love at your core. You don't need more of it; you just need to clear the clutter around your inherent source of love, which is YOU.

I have to credit Aaron Abke (endnote) for putting this into perfect language for me. He said,

"You cannot learn to love yourself because love is NOT a concept. The Ego wants a reason why it is lovable because of some quality or accomplishment. There is no reason.

Love is your reality. It's your true nature. It's not something to be learned, but rather something to be seen. To be aware of. To be realized.

And if you think to yourself, *If I am love, how come I can't feel love for myself?* The answer is that you DON'T know yourself. You are trying to love the not-self. Which does not exist.

True love is self-knowledge. So if you don't love yourself, that is only a sign that you are knowing yourself wrongly. You are living with a host of uninvestigated assumptions about who you are. Once these assumptions are investigated, they are quickly seen to be illusions that cover the true you. Love itself is what you are. You are the love you seek. Therefore self-love is simply the knowledge: "I am that."

If you feel like you don't love yourself, maybe that's okay right now. Maybe it's the most honest thing you could acknowledge because what you're really saying is that the YOU that you have evolved into is so far away from your natural state that you've blocked the flow of love. And if you can block it, you also hold the power to release the identities that are blocking you. If that's by spending time alone getting to recognize your own frequency and silencing all the distractions and voices you've had swirling around you, that's a great step to take. If it's confronting trauma with professional support, that can be a great step to take. But self-care isn't a checklist you can make and check off to experience self love. Healing isn't a formula. It's a journey.

HOW TO SPEND YOUR TWO HOURS

This book isn't my-way-or-the-highway. I'd be thrilled if as a reader these pages allowed you to rethink self-care and how it fits into your world. I feel like that would be a win. Please don't read this book as if it's a formula you have to follow.

In light of that, I want to be very conscious about how I tackle the number one thing I'm asked.

"What do you actually do in your two hours?!?"

I'm beyond happy to share with you on this, but I have one guideline I'd like to impose: Please do not follow this like a prescription. It's not. It's just what worked for me and things I got curious about as I looked for more things to do with my sacred time.

You and I are bound to be different. Hell, I bet we even like our eggs cooked differently. So don't just make them my way, feel free to cook them your way. How you'd spend your two hours will likely look different than how I'd spend mine. As you peek at the list I have included here, I guarantee there will be items on the list that will stand out as things you would never want to do. That's totally fine.

I truly believe that the magic of taking time each day to be alone is entirely based on how personalized and intentional you are with how you spend it.

That being said, here is a list of everything I tried in the first twelve months I spent two hours a day.

- Meditation
- Walking Meditation
- Grounding (aka bare feet in grass or dirt)
- Climbing trees
- Watching the ocean from on top of a cliff
- Hiking to the top of local peaks
- Watching the sun set
- Climbing up rocks
- Reading a book on enlightening topics
- Listening to audiobooks as I walked along the beach
- Journaling
- Automatic journaling
- Interpretive (or ecstatic) dance
- Tai chi style movements
- Stretching in the sunlight
- Dancing on a hilltop to spiritual music
- Sitting by a river, watching the water flow
- Body pendulum practice
- Pendulum practice
- Intuition practice
- Tarot card practice and interpretations
- Compassion meditation
- Listening to Reiki healing on YouTube

- Sensory deprivation floats
- Kundalini awakening meditations
- Sexual self-exploration
- Swinging on tree swings
- Silva method visualizations
- Watching animals in nature
- Asking for a sign through animals and then looking up the spiritual meanings of each animal I saw
- Asking for and collecting feathers on hikes
- Speaking out loud all my manifestations
- Embodying abundance as I walked through my future neighborhood, describing my future house
- Singing to spiritual music
- Chanting to balance my chakras
- Dancing to music in keys mapping to my chakras to help balance them
- Sound baths
- Swimming in the ocean
- Joining group coaching classes to develop my intuition and compassion
- Connecting to spirits, departed loved ones, and my intuition
- Channeling inspirational messages
- Practicing readings on close friends
- Napping in dire circumstances
- Gratitude journaling
- Rope flowing in nature
- Connecting to a high vibe friend
- Painting
- Adult coloring books while listening to sound healing music
- Swimming alone
- Enjoying a picnic outdoors

- You might be tempted to consider things like …
- Watching spiritual documentaries
- Podcasts (unless driving to a good hiking trail)
- Running self-love errands (even if it's something you think is buying you something out of self-care)
- Reading fiction

… but in my experience these ended up taking energy from me, not giving energy to my soul. The true litmus test is how you feel afterwards.

And let's notice what's NOT on my list that could very well make yours

- Workouts
- Dance class
- Art class
- Reading the Bible or another holy book
- Praying in the traditional sense
- Writing poetry
- Writing a song
- Cooking an incredible meal
- Writing letters
- Fly fishing
- Skateboarding
- Roller-skating
- Bouldering
- Cycling
- This list could be endless.

THE JOURNEY TO HAPPINESS

The basic concept I've landed on is this: The journey to happiness goes back to doing the things that brought us joy as children - Playing.

Learning. Exploring. Enjoying. And when we reconnect to this, we find that wellspring of joy and contentment we so often lose our grip on as adults, while we're chasing the obsession of having more.

Something magical happens when you carve out time each day to enjoy the life you work so hard to make for yourself. It's enough time to give you a physical, mental, and soulful reset. It's enough to remind you of the joy and blessing around you. It reminds you there is always more that is in control than out of control. It gives you the self-awareness you need to not overreact, because you know your next two-hour window to process your feelings is right around the corner. These two hours gives you the ability to jump off the hamster wheel of life and check in to see if you really want to continue to live life the way you've been doing it.

MY PROMISE REGARDING CHANGE

I will continue to evolve far beyond the pages of this book. The lessons and truths I discovered in this book are simply milestones in my journey to peace and contentment.

Thank you for joining me on my path. By finishing this book you stayed open and intrigued by how a simple habit could become a catalyst for a spiritual awakening and life transformation. Perhaps it reminded you of your own story. Maybe you needed to read mine to believe your own journey is possible. Either way, I thank you. Thank you for trusting my experience enough to give it some of your valuable time and energy.

My deepest dream is for my life to provide the canvas needed to paint inspiration and hope into the hearts of many. My pursuit will always be to keep infusing peace and happiness into my life and to share my personal journey in ways that encourage us all to create beautiful lives we're proud of. You are my people, and it is a privilege and joy to serve in any small way.

epilogue
MANIFESTO

I believe every one of us desires to find our true selves.

I believe until we do, our soul will never be at peace.

I believe to find yourself requires a process of unlearning every expectation, rule, stereotype that has too long defined you.

I believe we all possess the strength to strip down harmful conditioning and reclaim our identity and right to live on our own terms.

I believe experiencing happiness as an adult is not far removed from how we experienced happiness as a child.,

I believe most of us are chasing the wrong things, and deep down we not only know it, but we're actively trying to deny it.

I believe denying our soul's purpose manifests in sickness, illnesses in our bodies and minds.

I believe self-hatred is rooted in knowing all the layers of masks we've put on to protect ourselves are the very vices that imprison us in smallness.

I believe behind every hustler is a heart yearning for rest.

I believe behind every overachiever is a soul yearning for acceptance.

Behind every sharp tone or harsh word is a soul yearning for self kindness.

Behind every depressed spirit is a deep longing for freedom found through self permission to pursue what brings you joy.

Behind every angry mother is a woman who just wants to get it right and be a blessing to her family.

I believe each of us need to heal our own life experience as well as the wounds of our ancestors that we carry in our DNA.

I believe as humans we are obsessed with healing because we are collectively obsessed with triumph.

Most of all. I believe you are the only healer you need.

I believe your soul is deeply wise and holds the answers you seek.

I believe the greatest healing tools we have access to are dancing, laughing, nature, and solitude.

I believe the only way to succeed as a human doings is to try to ignore and silence your soul.

Because of this, I believe human doings perpetuate most of the struggles in this world.

I believe to be a happy human being is synonymous to being connected to ones soul and to cherish that connection.

I believe human beings were souls sent to this earth to help heal the planet and bring light to the world.

I believe when the world starts to value being over doing, it will mark a historic shift in consciousness.

I believe when we change ourselves by reconnecting to our souls, we send a ripple effect that permeates farther than we could have ever dreamt.

Because healing our families, our lineage, and ultimately our world only happens one soul at a time.

I believe when we identify with our soul before we identify with a mind or body, the healing journey begins.

I believe each of us are here for a unique purpose, one that begs to be discovered and followed.

I believe there are many paths to greatness and success but none so satisfying as following your intuition.

I believe intuition can only be heard in stillness, both silence from the noise and space to process free of scheduled demands.

I believe to reconnect to one's soul is a process of unlearning and relearning.

I believe to rewrite your own beliefs and discover the purest form of your identity takes time.

I believe intuition acts as a muscle that can be strengthened through consistent action and pure faith.

I believe the most powerful way to reconnect to yourself is to extract yourself from all the distractions and noise that's bombarded you for decades.

And I believe the secret to achieving all this can be found through making time to step away each day from all the demands of your life and tune into your soul to listen and follow.

bonus chapter
BLOOPER REEL

Okay I was laying in my bed, one week away from sending this manuscript to the publisher, when a sudden inspiration hit me: a blooper reel. I mean when I was going back through the archives of my memories to pick out the best experiences to describe various themes that I dove into in this book, I remembered some truly hilarious and ridiculous moments.

So if you're headed out into the sunset after reading this book, thinking you'll live happily ever after taking two hours... let me just say, expect some bloopers too.

Here's why. Because even if you are finally taking care of yourself, carving out that sacred time and feel like it's a truly magical moment, there are still moments where the coffee you drank fifteen minutes earlier has suddenly filled your bladder to the point of bursting, and you scramble off looking for the nearest bush out of sight from the trail you're hiking, only to remember you're wearing a bodysuit - a one piece bodysuit. And you are stranded with one of two options: you either fully undress to pee, or you have to grab the side of your one piece bodysuit and pull it far enough to the side to hopefully miss saturating it with urine and then having to feel and smell it the rest of the day.

So here are some stories that I wish had been filmed and some that I pray NO ONE actually saw in real life. Some are woo woo, some involve potty talk, and others just made me laugh out loud reliving.

BOULDER NUDGE

Okay so back when I was avidly pursuing opening that elusive third eye, I decided to hike on one of the peaks in my town. It takes about an hour and a half for me to hike up and down it, so another good reason to have two hours. Hikes like that become possibilities.

I hiked about two-thirds of the way up and then turned around and saw some incredible sun flares behind the marine layer rolling in. I felt called to climb on top of a small four foot tall boulder. For someone who did a lot of climbing in college, I have to say that NO ONE would have been able to tell that from watching me hump my way to the top of it. Damn those boulders with no holds, that look deceivingly simple and then you spend fifteen minutes tackling it and praying no one is watching you.

But I did it. I took it as a win.

Then I felt like I wanted to try to connect to the spirit world. I forget if it was Mother Mary or Jesus, but it was someone I was wanting to connect to. I listened to soft music, closed my eyes… while perched up on the side of a mountain, straddling a boulder, and I remember focusing so hard on trying to sense any connection to the spirit world.

It felt like an hour. I was disappointed.

I finally said out loud in my frustration: "Are you there? I can't sense anything. I may be new to this, but if there's any way to be a little more forceful, I'd appreciate it."

Be careful what you ask for. One second later, I felt an honest to God nudge from behind. Not the kind that could knock me off the boulder, thankfully, but like a friend is trying to get your attention.

Of course I looked behind me, and there was no one in sight, but it was an undeniable nudge.

I fist pumped the air. It was a huge validation to me. The spirit world was listening and wanted to connect.

I climbed down from the boulder, slightly scraping my backside as I descended. I didn't care. I was elated.

THAT'S MY MOM'S PEE JAR!

You already know I peed in a jar on day one of this whole journey. But what I haven't admitted yet is that the jar became a semi-permanent travel buddy. Semi simply because I frequently took it inside to wash it out so my car didn't start reeking like a porta-potty.

But during this time I would switch cars with one of our wonderful nannies, and she'd get to take the kids to fun outings like the zoo or the beach, and while in the beginning of this car swap, I was conscious about removing the infamous jar so as not to gross out our nanny, but like many things, you are on your best behavior for so long before you slip up.

One day I was made aware of this as I was back in my car, meditating and had to pee. Only I couldn't find the jar. Oh no! Where was it? I was reduced to peeing in nearby landscaping close to where I was parked.

When I got home, I saw the jar on the kitchen counter. Shoot! I hadn't remembered to bring it in. I felt embarrassment wash over me. I went over to it and quickly moved to put it away, when our nanny saw me and said, "I found that jar in your car, and I hope you don't mind, I washed it." "Oh thanks," I said, trying to be nonchalant.

And I almost got away with it too, until Kennedy walked into the kitchen and then said, "Aren't you glad we washed your pee jar?"

Silence.

TREE SWING MISHAP

Around the time I started to embrace that the process of healing is so often connected to playing again and doing things you loved as a child, I started to seek out tree swings. I'm happy to announce that San Luis Obispo has over a dozen amazing tree swings, and every time I discovered one, I felt like I had to christen it.

Not like a dog christens trees. Geez. I have pee jars for that.

But how a child does, by swinging on it.

One day I found a tree swing that was a literal bench tied up with climbing ropes on either side. It was about 4 feet from the ground, but beneath it were jagged sharp rocks. If you know where this is headed, then good for you. I was still categorizing this tree swing as secure and comfy. So I climbed up and brought my iPhone with me. The ropes were a little crooked, so I straightened them out.

This would be such a cool spot to meditate, I thought, feeling pretty secure in the tree swing.

So I turned on a nineteen minute guided YouTube meditation on manifesting my best life. I took a deep breath and let the soft Australian voice of the narrator bring me into my dream home and life. About seventeen minutes in, a thought darted strongly into my brain, "Get down now!"

I paused. Was that my intuition speaking in thought form?

"The swing is going to break!"

Oh shoot, that was real. I started to get down, one foot almost reaching the top of the jagged rocks, when one of the ropes broke and the swing went crashing down right on top of the sharp granite rocks. It had to have looked hilarious. I can't even describe what happened, but I was partially underneath the tree swing and partially on top of it. My legs were gashed, my iPhone case was cracked, and the fingers that had been clutching my phone were gashed so deeply I could see almost to the bone, and the blood hadn't even had a chance to flood in.

I wasn't even mad. I was thrilled. Why? Because my intuition tried to warn me! I had discovered a built in GPS for danger. Even though I hadn't obeyed it quickly enough, I had heard it and recognized it wasn't my own thoughts! The progress was a big win.

That being said, I had a bandaged middle finger for weeks, which was interesting to explain to clients. But that's the day I learned tree swings and meditation don't go well together.

DROP IT LIKE IT'S ... OUCH

While I had danced a decent amount growing up, I had sort of tabled it once I met Michael and stopped line dancing. However, alongside my experience with a kundalini awakening, I found dancing again. Not the kind that was choreographed and you're mentally following a basic eight count, but the kind of "go with the flow" sensual dancing I'd always wanted to do but had full on boycotted due to environmental objections. I just didn't want to try out dance moves I knew I had in me in a club where any sweat drenched horny human could see it as an invitation to grind up against me.

So I decided to try dancing in nature, somewhere no one could see.

At this point I was curating a playlist on Spotify called "Paden's Soul Music," and I had found someone else's playlist called Divine Feminine, so I decided I would hike to the top of the hill and dance to the music and see what happened.

Well, I got to the top and there was a group of moms laughing and gossiping about their kids' teacher. Nope. Not the vibe. So I decided to take one of secondary trails that clearly people rarely take, and I started to hike down a new side of the hill. Luckily, I found a labyrinth of side trails around the dry, pokey bushes that at that time of year looked like a nest of large tumbleweeds.

I was out of ear shot. I was out of eye sight. Feeling relatively confident that no one would be watching me figure out some intuitive dance moves, I started the playlist.

What unfolded was a solid hour of dancing to powerful, soulful music laced with ancestral beats. As the songs progressed, my moves got bolder. I had gotten my groove back.

Feeling inspired, I dropped it like it was hot … which would have been a cool move for sure, if it hadn't been for that spiky bush waiting for the opportunity to jolt me back to reality. Which it did, pierced me right through my leggings! Ouch!

HOLY WILDCAT

So around the time where I was starting to get obsessed with spirit animals, I began a habit of asking for spirit to show me new animals. Once day I said, "God, can you show me a new animal today?"

I tossed it up like a request and believed it would be treated as such.

I enjoyed my hike and let my mind wander, pondering deep philosophical meanings of things like life purpose and soul missions.

Ouch, I had a little stone in my shoe. I sat down next to a ditch used to direct water run off. I hike there almost every day, so I didn't think much of it.

Then I heard my intuition speak and say, "Look right."

I turned and not two feet from me was a bobcat, self grooming in the sunlight. Then it turned and we locked eyes. Oh shoot. I dropped my gaze remembering wild cats take eye contact as a challenge.

I slowly backed up, one shoe on and one shoe off, until I was far enough to safety to pull out my phone and check to the spiritual meaning of a bobcat.

"It's time for deep introspection."

I smiled and thanked God for the message and the new animal sighting. I'm a California native, and that was the first time I've seen a bobcat in real life. It was a powerful moment.

THAT SHITTY HIKE

I went through a phase where before every two-hour window of self-care, I would pull a card from a self-care deck I'd bought at a local crystal shop. I'd then incorporate whatever practice the card suggested (assuming it was practical).

You need to ground, put your barefoot on earth and let the energy of the earth ground and strengthen your root chakra.

Okay, simple enough. I left my shoes in my car, hit play on my binaural beats playlist, and headed out on a hike to ground.

I felt led to venture out away from the main trail. (Side note: is anyone noticing a theme here?) I was still barefoot, mind you, and that meant dealing with dry pokey weeds and side stepping sharp rocks. I spent so much time looking down at my feet. I was frustrated that I'd left my shoes in the car. Determined to enjoy the beauty of the hike, I found a meadow-like patch of natural grass and lifted my eyes up soaking up the views. Then my favorite song came on, and I just felt consumed by the audio and visual experience.

Then I did it.

I stepped right into a big fresh cow patty, so fresh it was still warm.

I nearly puked in my mouth. Thanks Mother Nature.

OFF KEY & LOUD

I went through a major Wayne Dyer phase, where I'd listen to a YouTube video of him teaching as I got ready in the morning and drove to wherever I was going to do my two hours. It always gave me new ideas and things to ponder.

One of the main things was the power of the sound "Om" and why chanting that particular sound is sacred for your body and soul. I thought I'd give it a try.

I got to a beautiful circle of trees off the side of the regular trail, far enough away to chant and not be disruptive, maybe.

I decided to be quiet. I couldn't pass up this circle of trees. They just looked so majestic.

So I climbed up one of the low hanging branches, straddling the massive limb. I hit play, and closed my eyes. I began chanting softly, or so I thought. It's hard to gauge when you've got ear phones in and the chanting has loud background music.

After a little while I heard voices and abruptly stopped. Three high-school aged boys were awkwardly looking at me and talking several yards away. They caught me looking at them and they burst into riotous laughter and ran away.

All my zen melted away.

SNOWY DRIFTS

Every year we go up to Lake Tahoe for Christmas week. It's one of our favorite traditions. And Michael and I alternate snowy walks! I had never meditated in the snow before, and while I wasn't excited about stopping to sit still in below 30 degree weather, I was open to a walking meditation.

I found one and started down the freshly snow plowed street.

I wandered, this time sticking to actual roads. I wasn't getting lost in the snow.

About half an hour in, I stood at the edge of Lake Tahoe. I stopped walking and stood right in the tree line, soaking in the beautiful view. I decided to make a snow man. I paused the meditation and tried to make an Olaf looking snowman to show my kids during our next snowy walk.

Whew! I was actually getting hot rolling and packing down this snowman's parts as I assembled it. I pushed back my fur lined hood and briefly took off my beanie.

That's when it happened.

The tree I was standing under, heavily laden with snow, dropped what felt like a wheelbarrow of snow right on my head. Fuck me.

DANCING WITH AN AUDIENCE

About a year into taking two hours a day, I started to realize I was creating a manifestation dance. I kept gravitating back to specific movements that went with my favorite song and specific meanings central to manifesting. I got so into it that I would close my eyes and just feel into the music and my body as it moved.

Once day I did this, and I went to the same spot I practiced this dance, and I got really into it. I mean eyes closed, picturing myself dancing in the cosmos. It was vivid.

I finished with a dramatic flourish, right as the song ended. Then I opened my eyes.

Not 2 feet from me stood a large black cow. We locked eyes. It just stared at me.

How long it had been there watching, I'll never know, but I'd have given anything for a pesky drone to have flown over and capture it.

ABOUT THE AUTHOR

Paden Hughes is a mom, author, CEO and public speaker who is passionate about helping ambitious empathetic leaders and entrepreneurs activate their dreams and align their lives to their soul purpose.